MORE GREAT ITALIAN PASTA

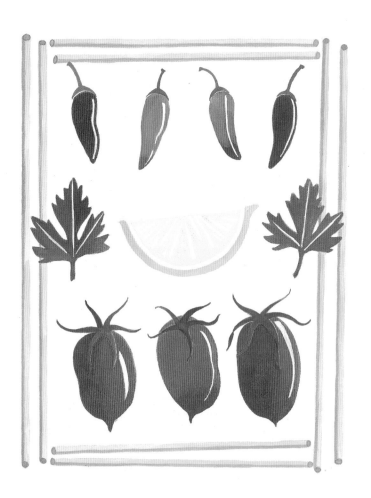

MORE
GREAT
ITALIAN
PASTA
DIANE SEED

Illustrated by Sarah Hocombe

SIMON & SCHUSTER

AUSTRALIA

*To Nicola, Caroline and Georgina,
and* il mio tesoro, *Alexander.*

MORE GREAT ITALIAN PASTA

First published in paperback in Australasia in 1993
First published in hardback in Australasia in 1992 by
Simon & Schuster Australia
20 Barcoo Street, East Roseville NSW 2069

A Paramount Communications Company
Sydney New York London Toronto Tokyo Singapore

© Text Diane Seed 1992
© Illustrations Sarah Hocombe

National Library of Australia
Cataloguing in Publication data

Seed, Diane.
   More great Italian pasta.

   Includes index.
   ISBN 0 7318 0425 2.

   1. Cookery (Pasta). 2. Cookery, Italian. I. Title.

641.822

Designed and illustrated by Helen Semmler
Typeset in Australia by Asset Typesetting Pty Ltd
Produced by Mandarin Offset in Hong Kong

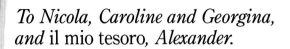

CONTENTS

INTRODUCTION

IN ITALY, EVERY REGION is justly proud of its culinary heritage and fine local produce, and traditional dishes are still prepared with love and skill. Often, a recipe varies from town to town, or family to family, but the common source remains obvious. Today there is also a 'new' style of cooking, often pioneered by local restaurants who have rediscovered old, forgotten recipes, or adapted firm favourites to make them lighter and more suited to the modern way of life. These new recipes use regional *materia prima* in fresh, exciting ways and have given an extra zest and vitality to Italian cooking. The ones I have happily included in this selection of recipes were created with care and a deep respect for local ingredients. They have nothing in common with some of the more bizarre offerings in which inappropriate ingredients are combined without rhyme or reason just for the sake of producing a new dish.

MAKING PASTA

In Italy, pasta is served as a first course, and in all the following recipes I have given quantities for six people eating pasta as a starter. If you intend to make the pasta the main dish you will need to increase the quantities, but make sure you do not inadvertently change the proportions.

Good dry Italian pasta is hard to beat, so there is really no need to make fresh pasta at home unless you want to experiment with unusual dough mixtures and interesting fillings.

Dry pasta should be cooked in a large, tall saucepan, using at least 4 L (7 pt) of water and 2 tablespoons of salt for 500 g (1 lb) of pasta. The water must be brought to a brisk boil and the salt dissolved before the pasta is added. Long pasta must be eased in gently and the pan should be partially covered to bring the water back to the boil as quickly as possible. The pasta should be stirred frequently with a wooden fork to keep the strands separate. You need to watch the pasta carefully so that it is not overcooked — no Italian would ever leave the kitchen while cooking pasta! Ignore any preconceived ideas about cooking time, and from time to time lift out and sample a small piece of pasta. The pasta is cooked when it is still firm in the centre and offers some resistance to the bite. In Italian this is known as *al dente*. Today there are splendid tall pasta pans with built in colanders that enable you to drain the pasta quickly with much less risk of scalding your hands and over-draining the pasta. The pasta should always be slightly shiny from the drops of water trapped between the coils, and a little pasta cooking water is often added to the sauce if it seems slightly dry.

In traditional trattorias you often see the cook tossing the freshly drained pasta into a large, heavy frying pan containing the sauce, his arm muscles rippling as he rotates the heavy pan to incorporate all of the pasta into his sauce. Most of us don't have a large enough frying pan, or enough muscle to emulate this very effective way of combining sauce and pasta, but I have discovered that a light, non-stick wok provides the perfect alternative. I make many sauces in my wok and the wider diameter makes it very easy to stir in the pasta, which can be served piping hot straight from the wok.

In order to make successful pasta dishes, good olive oil should be used and the Parmesan cheese should be bought in a piece and freshly grated for each recipe. It will keep for some time wrapped in foil and stored in the refrigerator. Some recipes call for the more pungent Pecorino cheese, but if this is unavailable use Parmesan. In all instances, if you cannot find a specific ingredient you should feel free to improvise and adapt the recipe. When anchovies are required you can use the whole anchovies preserved in salt, or the fillets in oil. Chillies vary in strength from plant to plant, and I even find the same plant is not always consistent. It is often better to dry some chillies and grind them up so that you begin to know the fire in your particular mixture.

FRESH PASTA

Fresh pasta is made at home in most regions of Italy.
Many traditional forms, such as the *pici* from Tuscany and the *orecchiette* from Puglia, use only flour and water. However, for most people, fresh pasta conjures up visions of the delicate golden pasta sheets made in Emilia Romagna using one egg to every 100 g (3½ oz) of flour. The flour is arranged in a mound on the table with a well in the centre. The eggs are broken into this well and a fork is used to draw the eggs gradually into the flour. A pinch of salt is sometimes added at this stage. Once all the egg has been worked into the flour the dough is kneaded by hand. If the mixture is too sticky a little more flour may be added. (It is not possible to be too precise because eggs vary in size and even flour mixtures vary

from country to country.) The pasta dough is kneaded energetically on a clean, floured surface using the heel of the hand, for ten minutes. If you are making large quantities it is easier to divide the dough into two or three balls and work separately, keeping the remaining balls covered with plastic film or kitchen foil. Some people prefer to use a food processor to make life easier.

The pasta is rolled out on a lightly floured large wooden board so that some moisture is absorbed, using a rolling pin about 80 cm (30 in) long. Alternatively the hand-cranked pasta machine makes it very easy to produce uniformly fine sheets. The pasta sheet is allowed to dry for about 30 minutes before being folded into a flat roll about 5 cm (2 in) wide and cut into the desired widths. These are then shaken out, arranged in little piles, and allowed to dry for at least 15 minutes.

If you intend to make stuffed pasta, the dough is made in the same way using two eggs and one egg yolk to 240 g (8 oz) flour and a pinch of salt. With stuffed pasta, the pasta sheet must not be allowed to dry. Either a fluted pastry wheel or a pastry cutter is used to cut out the desired shape, and it is necessary to work as quickly as possible. The cooking time will depend on the weight of the filling and the thickness of the pasta used so there is no hard and fast rule. You will have to keep testing.

TOMATO SAUCE

Many recipes call for a basic tomato sauce. There are countless regional variations, but this recipe is a fairly universal one.

2 x 400 g (12 oz) cans
Italian plum tomatoes
1 medium onion, finely
chopped
2 cloves garlic, finely
chopped
30 mL (2 tablespoons) olive
oil
Salt
Black pepper

Method: Heat the oil and gently fry the onion and garlic until soft. Add the tomatoes, with their juice, squashing them with the back of a wooden spoon. Cook uncovered over a high heat until the sauce thickens. Season to taste and pass through the medium disc of a food mill.

CRÊPES

Crêpes are often used in place of pasta to make an elegant starter, and many non-Italian cooks feel happier using this more familiar medium. The crêpes can be coated with a smooth filling, then rolled up in oblongs, or the filling can be arranged in the middle and the crepe folded into four to make a rounded three-cornered shape.

GNOCCHI

In the past, gnocchi were made with simple flour and water, and known as *maccheroni* like other forms of pasta. They were regarded as robust fare and often used as a neutral base to be served with meat and vegetable left-overs. After the potato was introduced into Europe, gnocchi began to be made with a combination of flour and floury potato, and for many years Italy has also had gnocchi made with semolina. Today many different vegetables are used with a small amount of flour to make light, tasty starters. Playing around with the traditional Italian vegetables to make unusual gnocchi is great fun. They are very simple to make in a food processor so are often an easy option.

VEGETABLES

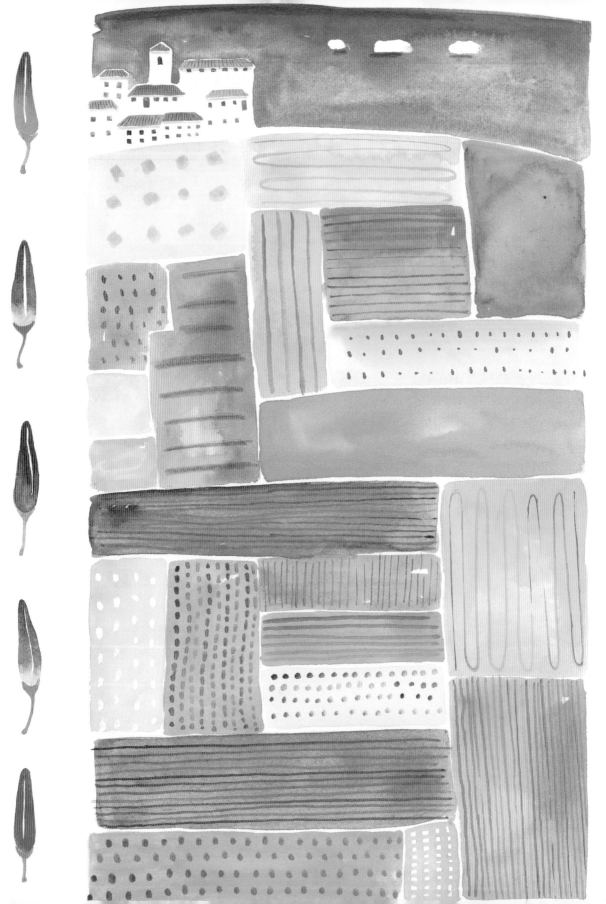

VEGETABLES

ITALY, WITH ITS VOLCANIC soil rich in minerals, produces some of the best vegetables in the world, and the combination of warm sunshine and fresh Mediterranean breezes gives an intense flavour to all the crops.

In every season, the market stalls are a constant source of temptation whether they are displaying tender mauve artichokes, opulent purple aubergines (eggplants), and lush, gaudy sweet peppers, or the more autumnal delights of orange pumpkin, tawny chestnuts and grotesque *funghi porcini*.

Many of the leafy green vegetables still grow wild on the hillsides, and the local women can often be seen patiently searching for these pungent treasures in the early morning before they wilt in the heat of the day.

The Italian *cucina povera* (the traditional cooking of the poor) has always relied heavily on these readily available herbs and vegetables and today, the more affluent society has also come to truly appreciate these pasta dishes based on one or two simple, perfect ingredients.

TAGLIATELLE WITH RICOTTA CHEESE AND FRESH HERBS

Tagliatelle alle erbe e ricotta

*60 g (2 oz) fresh herbs such as
    basil, tarragon, parsley and dill*
30 g (1 oz) shelled walnuts
500 g (1 lb) tagliatelle
Salt
*50 mL (3⅓ tablespoons) extra
    virgin olive oil*
250 g (8 oz) ricotta cheese
*60 g (2 oz) freshly grated pecorino
    cheese*
Black pepper

THIS LIGHT PASTA can be served cold in summer, but is even more delicious hot.

Method: Chop the herbs in a food processor. Add the nuts and process until they are reduced to very small pieces but not as small as crumbs.

Cook the pasta in boiling salted water and drain, reserving a ladle of the cooking water for the sauce if necessary. Stir in the oil, the nuts and herbs, the ricotta cheese and the pecorino. If the pasta seems too dry add a little pasta water. Season to taste.

FRESH PASTA WITH HERBS, TOMATO AND CHEESE

Maltagliati al pomodoro, erbette e robiola

500 g (1 lb) fresh pasta (or pappardelle)
45 mL (3 tablespoons) best quality extra virgin olive oil
1 shallot (spring onion/scallion), finely chopped
2 cloves garlic, finely chopped
3 ripe tomatoes, skinned, seeded and chopped into small cubes
Salt
Black Pepper
2 tablespoons fresh chopped herbs, including parsley, sage, rosemary and thyme
12 thin slices of fresh creamy cheese, like robiola della Langhe *made from goats' milk*

CLAUDIA VERRO SERVES this light pasta sauce at her lovely restaurant, La Contea, in Neive in Piedmont. In season, La Contea makes masterly use of the sumptuous white truffles. In this recipe, however, thin slices of fresh cheese are placed on top of the pasta imitating the slivers of truffles which adorn other pasta dishes. *Maltagliati* is pasta cut into uneven shapes and sizes. If you are making fresh pasta try Claudia's wickedly sinful proportions of 12 egg yolks and 400 g (12 oz) flour (see page 7 for method). Roll out the pasta thinly then cut into rough and uneven diamond shapes. If you are buying pappardelle break them into uneven lengths before cooking.

Method: Heat the oil and gently brown the shallot (spring onion/scallion) and garlic. Add the tomato cubes and heat through. Cook the pasta in boiling salted water. Stir the herbs into the tomato sauce while the pasta is cooking, leaving some for garnish. Drain the pasta, stir in the sauce, and arrange the cheese on top, dusted with the remaining herbs. Pour on a few drops of olive oil and serve at once.

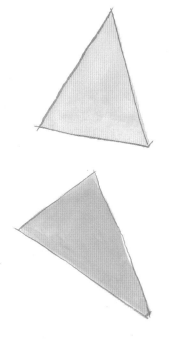

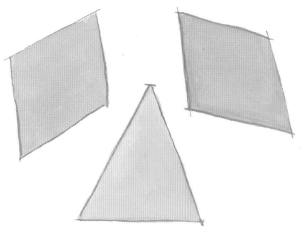

PENNETTE WITH ONIONS AND PARMESAN

Pennette alla Parmigiana e cipolla

100 g (3½ oz) butter
2 very large onions, finely chopped
Salt
Black pepper
500 g (1 lb) pennette
3 eggs, beaten
125 g (4 oz) freshly grated
*   Parmesan cheese*

THIS IS A deliciously different pasta which provides instant comfort on a cold day. It goes very well with a fine robust Chianti.

Method: Melt the butter and cook the onions slowly over a low heat until they are almost dissolved. Do not let the onions change colour. Season to taste. Keep warm while you cook the pasta in boiling salted water. When the pasta is nearly ready, return the onions to a low heat and stir in the beaten eggs. Remove from the heat. Drain the pasta and quickly stir in the cheese and the onion sauce. Serve at once.

RED BUTTERFLIES WITH PARMESAN

Farfalle alle barbabietole rosse

1 onion, finely chopped
75 g (2½ oz) butter
100 mL (3½ fl oz) dry white wine
500 g (1 lb) fresh beetroot, peeled,
    cooked and roughly chopped
15 mL (1 tablespoon) lemon juice
100 mL (3½ fl oz) cream
500 g (1 lb) farfalle
Salt
100 g (3½ oz) Parmesan cheese
Black pepper
1 tablespoon chopped mint

I USUALLY AVOID the butterfly-shaped pasta because I find either the middle is undercooked or the edges are overcooked. However this recipe looks so good I happily settle for the slightly undercooked centre.

Method: Cook the onion in one-third of the butter until soft then pour in the wine and cook for 3 minutes. Add the beetroot and cook for another 5 minutes. Allow to cool slightly then transfer to a food processor and purée with the lemon juice and cream. Cook the pasta in boiling salted water. Transfer the sauce into a large pan or wok and add the remaining butter. Drain the pasta and stir it into the sauce with the Parmesan. Season to taste and cook over a high heat for 3 minutes. Sprinkle on the mint and serve at once.

TAGLIATELLE WITH PEAS AND LETTUCE

Tagliatelle con lattuga e piselli

75 g (2½ oz) butter
1 small onion (or 1 shallot [spring onion/scallion], finely chopped
1 young crisp cos lettuce, cut into ribbons
300 g (9½ oz) shelled tender young peas
Salt
Black pepper
500 g (1 lb) tagliatelle

I LOVE THIS DELICATE pasta dish which always reminds me of the French way of cooking *petit pois* in a saucepan lined with lettuce leaves. It is delicious, even with frozen peas, and extra virgin olive oil can be substituted for butter for those wishing to avoid animal fats.

Method: Melt the butter and add the onion. When the onion is soft add the lettuce and the peas. Cover and cook gently until the peas are soft. Do not overcook or they will lose their lovely colour. Season to taste.

Cook the pasta in boiling, salted water, drain, reserving a little of the water for the sauce. Stir in the sauce, adding a little of the pasta water if the pasta seems too dry.

SEDANI WITH GREEN BEANS AND GORGONZOLA

Sedani con gorgonzola e fagolini verdi

500 g (1 lb) green beans
Salt
500 g (1 lb) sedani (or penne)
75 g (2½ oz) butter, diced
50 g (1½ oz) freshly grated
    Parmesan cheese
Black pepper
150 g (5 oz) Gorgonzola cheese,
    diced

ALTHOUGH THIS SAUCE works well with most pasta it looks best if you choose a short variety and cut the beans into lengths that match the pasta.

Method: Cook the beans in boiling salted water and drain while they are still firm and a good colour. Cook the pasta in boiling salted water, drain and stir in the butter and Parmesan cheese. Add a generous amount of black pepper. Gently stir in the beans and then the Gorgonzola. Serve at once.

SPAGHETTI WITH LEMON AND CHIVES

Bigoli al limone

2 large juicy lemons
25 blades of chives, chopped
2 tablespoons chopped parsley
75 mL (5 tablespoons) extra virgin
* olive oil*
Salt
Black pepper
500 g (1 lb) spaghetti

THIS SIMPLE, PASTA can be enjoyed by anyone wanting to avoid the usual lemon sauce with cream. *Bigoli* are made with wholewheat flour and water but they can be substituted with bought spaghetti.

Method: Grate the lemons, taking care not to use the bitter white pith. Squeeze out the juice and process the chives and parsley with the peel, juice and 15 mL (1 tablespoon) of the oil. Season to taste. Cook the pasta in boiling salted water, drain, and stir in the remaining oil. When the oil has been absorbed, stir in the sauce and serve at once. The pasta can be decorated with some threads of lemon peel.

SHELLS WITH VEGETABLES

Conchiglie alle verdura

2 medium-sized aubergines
(eggplants), diced
45 mL (3 tablespoons) olive oil
1 onion, finely chopped
2 cloves garlic, finely chopped
5 ripe tomatoes, peeled and seeded
Salt
Black pepper
150 g (5 oz) small green beans
1 sweet green pepper and 1 sweet
yellow pepper, seeded and cut
into small pieces
Oregano
500 g (1 lb) conchiglie
50 g (1½ oz) Parmesan cheese,
freshly grated

FRANCO COLOMBANI HAS a great collection of antique
cook books and a healthy respect for culinary
tradition, but he likes to experiment and use familiar
ingredients in new ways. In his lovely old Sole hotel
in Maleo, near Parma, he combines typical
Mediterranean vegetables with his regional glory,
Parmesan cheese.

Method: Cover the diced aubergine (eggplant) with
salt and leave for 1 hour to purge its bitter liquid.
Heat half the oil and gently cook the onion, garlic,
tomatoes and rinsed and dried aubergine (eggplant).
Season to taste. Cook the beans in boiling salted
water until they are not quite tender. Heat the
remaining oil and cook the sweet peppers with the
oregano and a little salt. Mix the drained beans with
all the other vegetables and cook for 5 minutes.

Cook the pasta in boiling salted water, drain and
stir in the Parmesan and vegetables. Serve at once.

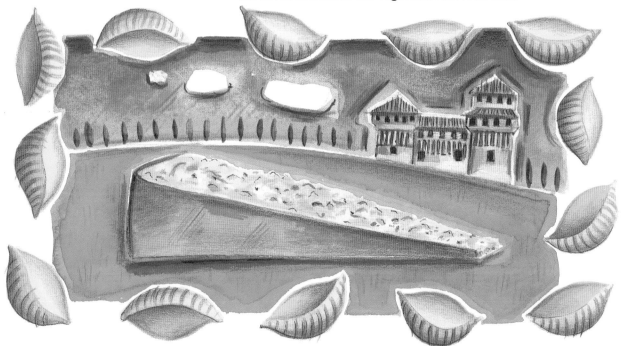

SICILIAN AUBERGINE (EGGPLANT) DELIGHTS
Delizie di Trinacria

6 large aubergines (eggplants)
Salt
250 g (8 oz) linguine
300 g (9½ oz) fresh ricotta cheese
500 mL (16 fl oz) fresh tomato
  sauce (see page 8)
Black pepper
6 large, thin slices caciocavallo
  cheese or any cheese that will
  melt to coat the layers of
  aubergine (eggplant)
6 small tomato slices
6 small sprigs basil

TOTUCCIO CASCINO GIVES traditional local ingredients a new slant in his Monreale restaurant, La Botte. Sicily's historic name, Trinacria (meaning 'three-cornered'), is used to name this original aubergine (eggplant) pasta. The dish is presented in two perfect mounds. This is reminiscent of the famous cakes produced by Sicilian nuns and popularly known as *minni di vergini* or 'virgins' breasts', because they were small, firm and white. Sicilian nuns were famous for their intricate cakes and biscuits, and even closed orders made extravagant delicacies for sale to the outside world.

Method: Cut the aubergines (eggplants) into 24 slices about 1 cm (⅓ in) thick (two mounds each for six people). You will need a base and a slightly smaller top slice for each mound to give the right cone shape. Cover the aubergine (eggplant) slices with salt and leave for an hour to purge their bitter juices. Rinse off the salt, dry then grill on both sides until they are cooked. Cook the linguine in boiling salted water until they are only three-quarters cooked, drain and stir in the ricotta and the tomato sauce. Adjust seasoning. For each mound arrange a layer of coiled linguine between the two aubergine (eggplant) slices, and drape the thin slice of cheese over the top and sides. Cook in a hot oven at 230°C (450°F) until the cheese has melted to coat the little aubergine (eggplant) and pasta mounds. Garnish the top with a small slice of tomato and sprig of basil.

AUBERGINE (EGGPLANT) BOATS STUFFED WITH PASTA

Barchette di melanzane

6 plump aubergines (eggplants)
Salt
Black pepper
30 mL (2 tablespoons) olive oil
750 mL (1¼ pt) fresh tomato sauce
(see page 8)
Oil for frying the aubergine casing
400 g (12 oz) tubetti or cannolicchi
100 g (3½ oz) freshly grated
Parmesan cheese
100 g (3½ oz) mozzarella cheese,
diced
12 basil leaves for decoration

IN THE SOUTH of Italy *melanzane* are used in myriad ways to make enticing pasta dishes. These attractive, ingenious little 'boats' make a good starter for a dinner party. They can be prepared in advance and put in a hot oven at the last minute.

Method: Cut the stalks off the aubergines (eggplants), lay them lengthwise and slice off the top third of each. This part should be cut into cubes and covered with salt for 30 minutes to purge the bitter juice. With a curved knife carve out the flesh from the larger segments, being careful not to spoil the shape or cut the skin. Chop the flesh into small cubes, and put to purge with the rest of the aubergines (eggplants). Rinse off the salt and pat dry.

Heat the oil and gently cook the diced aubergine (eggplant) for 5 minutes. Add the tomato sauce and keep warm. In enough oil to coat the pan, fry the aubergine (eggplant) 'shells' with the skin upwards so that they are pliable without being too soft to handle. Cool on paper towel to remove any excess oil.

Place the pasta in boiling salted water then remove from heat while still slightly undercooked and drain. Stir in the mozzarella, the sauce and the Parmesan cheese. Spoon the mixture into the aubergine (eggplant) casings, place on a tray and cook in a hot oven (250°C/500°F) for 5-10 minutes. Decorate with the basil leaves then serve at once.

SMALL 'RAGS' OF EGG PASTA

Stracci di pasta alle mille erbe

*A large bunch of fresh herbs, finely
chopped (include, if possible,
parsley, mint, basil, thyme,
tarragon and marjoram)*
*60 mL (4 tablespoons) extra virgin
olive oil*
Salt
Black pepper
500 g (1 lb) egg pasta
*100 g (3½ oz) freshly grated
Parmesan or pecorino cheese*

THE LOCANDA DELL' AMOROSA is a magical hotel in
Tuscany occupying the buildings of an entire
medieval village. The steep, narrow approach road is
lined by an avenue of cypress trees and leads to a
tranquil, comfortable retreat that seems to belong to
a more leisurely era. The restaurant serves a
judicious mixture of old and new Tuscan recipes and
this speciality makes full use of the well-stocked herb
garden.

Method: Stir the herbs into the oil with salt and
pepper. Cook the pasta in boiling salted water taking
care not to overcook, drain well then toss in the
cheese and the oil and herbs. Serve at once.

SPAGHETTI WITH GARLIC

Spaghetti con aglio

12 cloves garlic, peeled
100 mL (3½ fl oz) olive oil
Salt
500 g (1 lb) spaghetti
1 tablespoon chopped parsley

I THINK THIS IS ONE of the best recipes from the Neapolitan *cucina povera* tradition and it is served to perfection on the island of Ischia at the Sant'Angelo restaurant, Girasole. It is simple and very inexpensive, but the secret lies in never taking your eyes off the garlic when it is cooking. It needs to be a pale creamy beige and a few seconds too long in the oil will spoil the flavour and give a bitter taste.

Method: Dice the garlic into small, even cubes, do not use a garlic squeezer or mincer. Heat the oil and fry the garlic until it begins to change colour and then use a slotted spoon to remove *immediately* from the hot oil. Cook the pasta in boiling salted water, drain and stir in the oil, garlic and parsley.

TAGLIATELLE WITH LEEKS

Tagliatelle con porri

4 leeks
30 g (1 oz) butter
Freshly ground black pepper
45 mL (3 tablespoons) light stock
180 mL (6⅓ fl oz) cream
Salt
500 g (1 lb) tagliatelle
75 g (2½ oz) freshly grated
   Parmesan cheese

PIEDMONT HAS MANY traditional recipes using leeks in soups and risotto, but this recipe is a new variation from chef, Cesare Giaccone, who has a restaurant in the Langhe region. He adds a little Parmesan cheese to the dough when he is making his fresh pasta for this dish but it works equally well with the more usual egg pasta, fresh or dry.

Method: Using only the white and light green parts of the leeks, chop into thin rings. Melt the butter and cook the leeks gently with a little freshly ground black pepper. When the leeks are soft add the stock and cream and simmer gently for 20 minutes. Check the seasoning. Cook the pasta in boiling salted water, drain and stir in the leek sauce and Parmesan cheese. Serve at once.

PENNE WITH HAZELNUTS

Penne con le nocciole

*45 mL (3 tablespoons) extra virgin
  olive oil*
1 clove garlic
*1 pinch ground chilli or cayenne
  pepper*
*125 g (4 oz) shelled hazelnuts,
  finely chopped*
500 g (1 lb) penne or sedanini
Salt
*75 g (2½ oz) freshly grated
  Parmesan cheese*
Black pepper

PIEDMONT HAS MANY traditional recipes using hazelnuts. This is an unusual new pasta dish using the same ingredient.

Method: Heat the oil, add the garlic clove and allow it to turn golden brown. Add the chilli and nuts, cook for a few minutes, then remove the garlic. Cook the pasta in boiling salted water, drain and stir in the cheese and the nuts. If the pasta seems too dry, stir in a ladle of pasta water before serving. Season to taste and serve at once.

PENNE WITH JULIENNED CARROTS AND CELERY

Penne con sedano e carote

45 mL (3 tablespoons) extra virgin olive oil
2 cloves garlic, minced
3 celery sticks, cut into thin strips
3 carrots, cut into thin strips
Salt
Black pepper
500 g (1 lb) penne
50g (1½ oz) freshly grated Parmesan cheese (optional)

IN ITALY WHEN YOU buy your vegetables you are usually given a free bunch of *odori*, which consists of 1 or 2 celery stalks, carrots and a few fresh herbs. These basic ingredients can be found in most Italian kitchens so this easy pasta dish is often made when the cupboard is otherwise bare!

Method: Heat the oil and gently cook the garlic, celery and carrots until soft. Season to taste. Cover and keep warm. Cook the pasta in boiling salted water, drain and stir in the vegetables. If you are using Parmesan cheese stir into the pasta before adding the sauce. Serve at once.

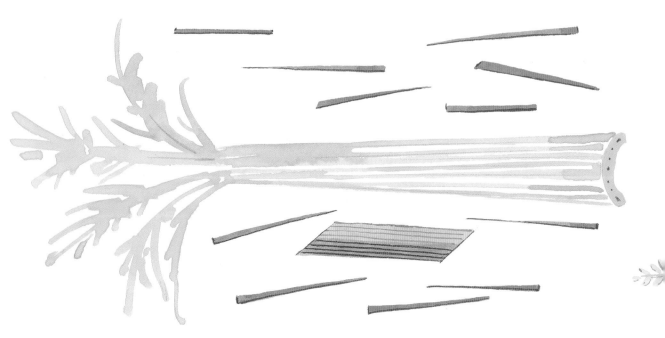

TAGLIOLINI WITH CREAMED CARROTS

Tagliolini alla crema di carote

500 g (1 lb) carrots
Salt
100 mL (3½ fl oz) cream
Pinch of nutmeg and cinnamon
100 g (3½ oz) freshly grated
    Parmesan cheese
Freshly ground black pepper
500g (1 lb) tagliolini
50 g (1½ oz) butter cut into small
    cubes

THIS IS A SIMPLE economical dish which can be easily prepared. The golden sauce looks very attractive with pale green pasta.

Method: Cook the carrots in boiling salted water, drain and purée. Blend in the cream, spices and half the cheese. Season to taste. Cook the pasta in boiling salted water, drain and stir in the butter, remaining cheese and carrot sauce. Add a little freshly ground black pepper and serve at once.

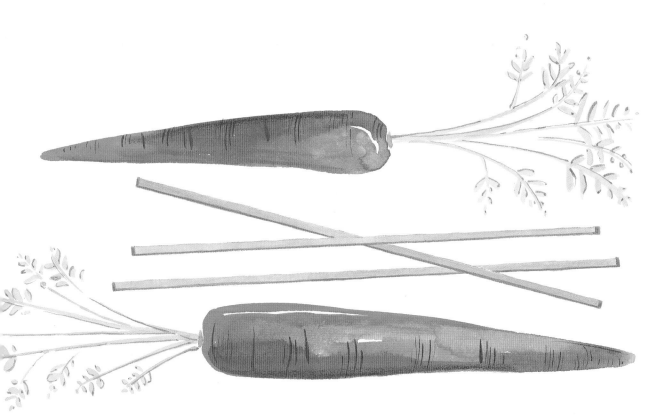

PASTA WITH CEPS

Pici in salsa di porcini

400 g (12 oz) fresh ceps
30 g (1 oz) butter
30 mL (2 tablespoons) extra virgin
 olive oil
2 cloves garlic, finely chopped
Salt
Black pepper
1 tablespoon chopped parsley
500 g (1 lb) pici, spaghetti or penne

IN TUSCANY THE traditional pasta *pici* is made by hand using one egg to about 800 g (1¾ lb) flour. The dough is worked energetically with a little oil and water to make it very elastic and then pulled and rolled to make long, thick strings. The art is passed from mother to daughter. The real experts produce *pici* that are often over 1 m (3 ft) long. Spaghetti or penne can be used in place of *pici*, but not egg pasta. This recipe cannot be made with dried ceps.

Method: Scrape any soil off the mushrooms and wipe with a damp sponge. Do not immerse in water or they will become soggy. Cut into fine slices. Heat butter and oil and cook mushrooms slowly for 10 minutes. Add the garlic, season to taste and then sprinkle on the parsley. Cook the pasta in boiling salted water, drain, and stir in the sauce. Serve at once.

FRESH PASTA MADE WITH DRIED CEPS

Fettuccine fresca con funghi porcini nel impasto

50 g (1½ oz) dried ceps
About 25 rosemary 'blades',
carefully removed from the sprig
6 eggs
500 g (1 lb) flour
15 mL (1 tablespoon) olive oil
100 mL (3½ fl oz) dry white wine
Semolina to sprinkle on fresh pasta
sheets
Salt
50 g (1½ oz) butter
100 g (3½ oz) freshly grated
Parmesan cheese
Black pepper

IT IS WORTH the extra effort to make this fresh pasta with the ceps worked into the dough. The cooked pasta is tossed in butter and Parmesan cheese to enhance the good mushroom flavour.

Method: Soak the ceps in tepid water for 10 minutes. Change the water and soak for another 10 minutes. Drain and process with the rosemary spikes to make a smooth cream.

To make the pasta dough, work the eggs into the flour, then work in the oil and then the ceps mixture. Add enough wine to make a pliable dough and knead energetically until soft and elastic. This can be done by hand or in a food processor. Divide into four balls and keep three balls covered as you roll out the first one into a sheet. Sprinkle the sheet with semolina then roll up to make a scroll. Cut into rings about ½ cm (⅕ in) wide. When all the pasta has been cut up, shake out the rings and arrange them in little piles. Leave for at least an hour, uncovered, so that the pasta dries out a little. The pasta can be left for longer if it is more convenient.

When ready to eat, cook in boiling salted water, drain and stir in the butter and cheese. Sprinkle a little freshly ground pepper on top.

1

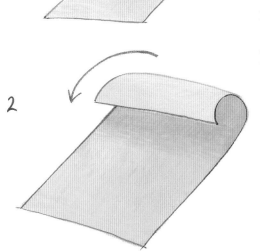

2

3

4

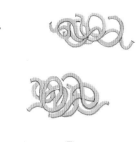

TAGLIATELLE CROWNED WITH CEPS

Tagliatelle con testa di porcini

1 large lemon
1 tablespoon finely chopped parsley
1 clove garlic, minced
30 mL (2 tablespoons) extra virgin
     olive oil
6 caps of fresh ceps
100 mL (3½ fl oz) dry white wine
15 mL (1 tablespoon) lemon juice
Salt
500 g (1 lb) tagliatelle

IF YOU HAVE SOME beautiful ceps this recipe shows them off in all their glory, since the *funghi porcini* (cep), instead of being sliced in the usual way, is kept whole and each serving is embellished with a mushroom crown.

Method: Grate the lemon peel, being careful not to use the bitter white pith, and mix with the parsley and garlic. Clean the ceps with a damp sponge. Heat the oil and brown the ceps quickly on each side. Pour in the white wine, add the lemon juice and lemon peel mixture and keep warm while the pasta is cooking.

Cook the pasta in boiling salted water and drain. Carefully lift the ceps out of their cooking liquid and toss the pasta in this sauce. Arrange a cep on top of each portion and serve at once.

TAGLIATELLE WITH CHANTERELLE SAUCE

Tagliatelle con salsa di finferli

*400 g (12 oz) chanterelle
   mushrooms*
50 g (1½ oz) butter
15 mL (1 tablespoon) olive oil
*1 shallot (spring onion/scallion),
   sliced*
Salt
Black pepper
1 tablespoon chopped parsley
500 g (1 lb) green tagliatelle

I LOVE THE LOVELY golden yellow chanterelle mushrooms and they make a spectacularly pretty sauce for this quick, easy dish. Do not substitute other mushrooms in this dish as they are not as flavoursome as chanterelles.

Method: Brush the soil off the mushrooms and wipe clean with a damp cloth. Do not wash by immersing in water or you will ruin the taste and texture of the mushrooms. Slice the mushrooms. Heat the butter and oil and gently fry the shallot (spring onion/scallion) until soft. Add the mushrooms and cook on a low heat for a few minutes. Season to taste and add the parsley. Keep warm while you are cooking the pasta in boiling salted water. Drain and stir in the sauce. Serve at once.

THICK AND THIN PASTA WITH NETTLES

Pappardelle e tagliolini con l'ortica

750 g (1½ lb) tender nettle leaves
Salt
75 g (2½ oz) butter
400 g (12 oz) pappardelle
100 g (3½ oz) tagliolini
75 g (2½ oz) freshly grated
   Parmesan cheese
Black pepper

THE TWO PASTAS need to be cooked separately for this unusual dish but the end result is worth the effort. The tender new leaves of nettles are used to give a subtle flavour, but if you can't find nettles try substituting sorrel or any other leafy green vegetable.

Method: Cook the nettle leaves in boiling salted water quickly. The moment they become soft, drain and plunge into iced water to keep them from discolouring. Chop finely in a food processor then put in a large pan or wok with two-thirds of the melted butter.

Cook the two pastas separately in boiling salted water. The pappardelle will take longer to cook than the tagliolini. Drain the pappardelle, stir into the nettle sauce and add two-thirds of the cheese. Stir vigorously over a low heat for a couple of minutes. Toss the drained tagliolini in the remaining butter and cheese and add a little black pepper. Portion out the pappardelle on individual plates. Arrange the tagliolini in a small mound on top. Serve at once.

SUN TAGLIATELLE

Tagliatelle del Sole

500 g (1 lb) tagliatelle
Salt
100 g (3½ oz) butter
6 eggs
75 g (2½ oz) freshly grated
  Parmesan cheese
80 g (2¾ oz) white truffle, cut into
  slivers

THIS RECIPE WAS perfected by Franco Colombani for his Maleo hotel, Albergo del Sole. The egg yolk on top of the pasta looks like a great yellow sun and flecked pale beige slivers of white truffles add the crowning touch. The recipe can be prepared without truffles by adding any garnish that takes your fancy. You have to move very quickly when assembling this dish so that the eggs do not congeal or the pasta get cold.

Method: While the pasta is cooking in boiling salted water, melt the butter and gently break the eggs into it. I cook two at a time in order to keep them separate. Salt lightly and fry until set. Do not let the white become brown. Remove the eggs carefully with a slotted spoon, keeping the butter to dress the pasta. Cut off the whites using a pastry cutter. Drain the pasta and stir in the Parmesan cheese. Arrange the pasta on individual plates with the egg yolk and melted butter on top. Place the slivers of truffles or alternative garnish around the egg yolk like rays. Serve at once.

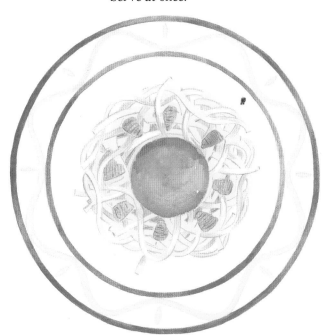

TAGLIATELLE WITH FONTINA CHEESE AND WHITE TRUFFLE

Tagliatelle con fontina e tartufo bianco

White truffle
100 g (3½ oz) butter
100 g (3½ oz) fontina cheese, cut
*   into small cubes*
25 mL (1⅔ tablespoons) light stock
Salt
Black pepper
500 g (1 lb) tagliatelle

PASTA PROVIDES THE ideal neutral base for the opulent white truffle, allowing the full flavour to be savoured without distraction. White truffles cost a king's ransom, but a very little goes a long way and they turn pasta into an ambrosial feast. White truffles should never be cooked so be careful to remove the sauce from the heat before you add the truffle.

Method: Scrape any soil off the truffle then shave off one thin slice. Put this aside and slice the rest of the truffle for decoration. (There is a special utensil for slicing truffles, but I find my sharp vegetable knife much easier to control.) Melt the butter and add the cheese and the stock so that the cheese becomes sufficiently fluid. Add a pinch of salt if required, and freshly ground black pepper. Remove the sauce from the heat, crumble the first truffle slice and stir it into the sauce. Cook the pasta in boiling salted water, drain and stir in the sauce. Decorate the pasta with the wafer-thin slices of truffle and serve at once.

BAKED TAGLIOLINI WITH BLACK TRUFFLE

Tagliolini con tartufo nero al forno

100 g (3½ oz) black truffle
500 g (1 lb) tagliolini
Salt
100 g (3½ oz) butter, melted
2 eggs, beaten
100 g (3½ oz) freshly grated
   Parmesan cheese
Black pepper

BLACK TRUFFLES, UNLIKE white truffles, are usually cooked to extract all their flavour. This simple baked pasta from Umbria is a perfect dinner party treat.

Method: Scrape any mud off the truffle then cut it into wafer-thin slices. Cook the pasta for about 2–3 minutes in boiling salted water then drain. In a buttered oven dish arrange one-third of the pasta and cover with one-third each of the butter, eggs and cheese. Arrange half the truffle slices on top then cover with half the remaining pasta. Spoon over half the remaining butter, eggs and cheese and arrange all the rest of the truffle on top. Make a third layer of pasta, cover with the remaining butter, eggs and cheese and grind on some black pepper. Bake in a 250°C (500°F) oven until golden brown. Serve at once.

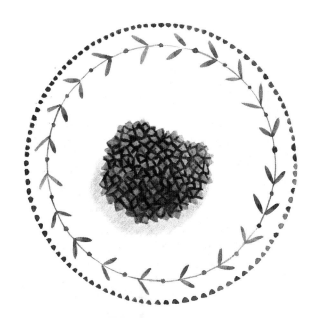

LINGUINE DEVIL'S FASHION

Linguine dei diavoli

45 mL (3 tablespoons) olive oil
1 onion, chopped
2 cloves garlic, chopped
1 hot red chilli pepper
6 large sweet red peppers, seeded
    and roughly chopped
3 ripe tomatoes, fresh or tinned,
    chopped
Salt
Black pepper
Cayenne pepper to taste (optional)
500 g (1 lb) linguine

THIS PASTA GETS its devilish name from the very small hot red chillies known as *diavolicchi* or little devils.

Method: Heat the oil and gently cook the onion and garlic. As they begin to change colour add the chilli, red peppers and tomatoes. Cook until the vegetables are soft, remove the chilli and then pass through a food mill. Check the seasoning and add a little cayenne pepper if the sauce is too bland. Cook the pasta in boiling salted water, drain and stir in the sauce. Serve at once.

SPAGHETTI WITH SUN-DRIED TOMATOES

Spaghetti con i pomodori secchi

50 mL (3⅓ tablespoons) olive oil
1 small onion, finely chopped
1 celery stick, chopped
*250 g (8 oz) sun-dried tomatoes,
    chopped*
*300 g (9½ oz) fresh or canned red
    tomatoes, skinned, seeded and
    chopped*
Salt
Black pepper
500 g (1 lb) spaghetti

IN THE HOT SOUTH, Italians open the tomatoes and dry them in the sun. The dried tomatoes are then preserved in olive oil with various aromatics, such as garlic, chilli peppers, capers or basil, giving them a very intense flavour. They are now exported all over the world. They add 'a beaker full of the warm south' to a simple tomato sauce.

Method: Heat the oil and add the onion. When this is soft add the celery and sun-dried tomatoes. Stir and cook for about 5 minutes then add the fresh or canned tomatoes. Cook quickly over a high heat until you have a thick sauce. Season to taste, using salt with caution because the sun-dried tomatoes are usually quite salty. Cook the pasta in boiling salted water, drain and stir in the sauce. Cheese can be served separately if desired.

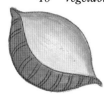

LARGE SHELLS STUFFED WITH CAULIFLOWER SOUFFLÉ

Conchiglioni ripieni di soffiato di broccolo

1 cauliflower
15 mL (1 tablespoon) olive oil
1 onion, chopped
40 g (1⅓ oz) pine nuts
40 g (1⅓ oz) sultanas
2 anchovy fillets, rinsed and
    chopped
Salt
Pepper
75 g (2½ oz) butter
36 large shells or 'snails'
    (6 per person)
3 egg whites, stiffly beaten

THIS NEW RATHER than traditional recipe can be made with your favourite vegetable, but if you don't use broccoli or cauliflower omit the pine nuts, sultanas and anchovies which are only combined with broccoli and cauliflower in traditional Sicilian dishes. It is important to use shells or *lumaconi* (large snails) because the beaten egg whites make the filling puff up to form little soufflés.

Method: Cook the cauliflower in boiling salted water. Drain and reserve a ladle of cauliflower water. Divide into florets and keep warm.

Heat the oil and gently cook the onion until soft. Add the nuts and sultanas, stir well and then add the cauliflower. After 2 minutes pour in a ladle of cauliflower water and the anchovy fillets. When the anchovy has almost 'melted', season to taste and purée the mixture, adding 50 g (1½ oz) of melted butter. Cook the pasta shells in boiling salted water until they are pliable but not soft. Drain. When the cauliflower mixture is cool, fold in the egg whites. With a teaspoon or forcing bag fill the pasta shells and arrange in an oven dish greased with the remaining butter. Cook in an oven at 225°C (430°F) until the filling has risen and the pasta is golden brown.

BAKED LARGE SHELLS STUFFED WITH WATERCRESS

Conchiglioni con ricotta e crescione

FILLING

30 g (1 oz) butter
1 shallot (spring onion/scallion),
*   sliced*
400 g (12 oz) watercress leaves
300 g (9½ oz) ricotta cheese
2 egg yolks
75 g (2½ oz) freshly grated
*   Parmesan cheese*
Grated nutmeg
Salt
Black pepper
400 g (12 oz) large shells

BECHAMEL SAUCE

50 g (1½ oz/4 tablespoons) flour
50 g (1½ oz) butter, melted
1 L (1¾ pt) hot milk
Salt
Black pepper

ANY LARGE DRY pasta shape can be used to make this recipe and the pasta can be stuffed in advance and baked in its sauce at the last minute.

Method: To make the filling heat the butter and gently cook the shallot (spring onion/scallion) until soft. Add the watercress, stir for 2–3 minutes then leave to cool. Beat together the ricotta, egg yolks and Parmesan cheese. Season to taste with a little nutmeg, salt and pepper.

Cook the shells in boiling salted water until pliable but not soft.

To make the sauce, stir the flour into the butter and cook for 3 minutes. Gradually add the milk and stir until smooth. Season to taste and cook for 10 minutes.

Grease an oven dish and cover with a thin coating of sauce. Fill the shells, arrange in the dish and cover with the remaining sauce. Bake at 220°C (425°F) for 10 minutes. Serve at once.

LARGE HERB RAVIOLI FILLED WITH TOMATO AND MOZZARELLA

Ravioli giganti ripieni di pomodori e mozzarella

PASTA

3 eggs
30 g (1 oz) butter, melted
2 cloves garlic, finely chopped
1 tablespoon finely chopped
  rosemary
1 tablespoon finely chopped thyme
Salt
Pepper
450 g (14½ oz) flour

FILLING

100 g (3½ oz) tomatoes, peeled,
  seeded and finely chopped
100 g (3½ oz) mozzarella cheese,
  diced
1 tablespoon basil leaves cut into
  fine strips
Salt
Black pepper

50 g (1½ oz) butter, melted
50 g (1½ oz) freshly grated
  Parmesan cheese
12 sprigs basil

A COMBINATION OF fresh herbs makes an interesting pasta dough that can be used for many fillings. Here it gives an original flavour to the long-time favourite tomato and mozzarella.

Method: To make the pasta, beat the eggs and add the melted butter, garlic, herbs and seasoning. Gradually work in the flour, adding a little water if necessary. Roll out the pasta to a sheet ½ cm (⅕ in) thick and cut out 12 large squares about 10 x 8 cm (4 x 3 in). This will give one giant ravioli per serving. Cover the pasta while you are making the filling.

To make the filling, mix together all the ingredients. Let the mixture stand for about 1 hour to allow the flavours to blend. Season to taste. Arrange the filling on six squares and cover with the remaining squares, sealing the edges well. Cook in boiling salted water for about 10 minutes. Lift out with a slotted spoon and dress with melted butter and cheese. Arrange 2 sprigs of basil on top of each ravioli. Serve at once.

ROCKET RAVIOLI IN BASIL SAUCE

Ravioli di rucola alla crema di basilico

PASTA

600 g (1 lb 4 oz) flour
180 mL (6 fl oz) tepid water
2 eggs
1 egg yolk
A dash of dry white wine (optional)

FILLING

1.2 kg (2½ lb) Swiss chard, spinach
  or borage
600 g (1 lb 4 oz) rocket leaves
Salt
Black pepper
225 g (7½ oz) ricotta cheese or
  thick yoghurt
3 eggs
75 g (2½ oz) freshly grated
  Parmesan cheese
30 g (1 oz) butter
¼ teaspoon nutmeg

SAUCE

300 g (9½ oz) basil leaves
150 g (5 oz) pine nuts (walnuts or
  almonds can be substituted)
200 g (6½ oz) freshly grated
  Parmesan
100 mL (3½ fl oz) extra virgin
  olive oil
50 mL (3⅓ tablespoons) fresh
  cream
Salt
Pepper

THIS IS A DELICIOUS new Ligurian recipe from the restaurant Il Giardino dei Glicini in Genoa.

Method: Make the fresh pasta (see page 7), roll out and cut into 12 or 18 diamonds (two or three ravioli per person).

To make the filling cook the greens in boiling salted water, drain well, then process with the other ingredients to make a smooth paste.

Spoon a little filling onto half of each diamond then fold over to form a triangle, sealing the edges well.

To make the sauce, process all the ingredients together to form a smooth, creamy mixture.

Cook the pasta in boiling salted water for about 10 minutes. Remove with a slotted spoon and stir in the sauce. Serve at once.

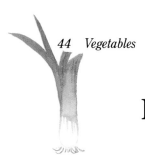

BEETROOT TAGLIATELLE WITH LEEK SAUCE

Tagliatelle alla barbietola con salsa di porri

PASTA

600 g (1 lb 4 oz) flour
6 eggs
30 mL (2 tablespoons) olive oil
A pinch salt
1 small, fresh beetroot, peeled,
  cooked and puréed

SAUCE

30 g (1 oz) butter
3 leeks, sliced into fine rings
200 mL (7 fl oz) cream
Salt
Black pepper
70 g (2¼ oz) freshly grated
  Parmesan cheese

A SMALL, COOKED beetroot is used to turn the fresh pasta dough a deep pink which contrasts with the pale green leeks.

Method: Make the pasta by working together the flour, eggs, oil and salt. When you have a smooth dough add the beetroot and work evenly into the dough. Roll out the dough into a fine sheet, roll up like a scroll, and cut into fine rings. Shake out the strings of tagliatelle, arrange in little heaps, and leave out uncovered for about 30 minutes to dry.

Melt the butter in a pan and gently cook the fine rings of leeks until they are soft. Pour in the cream, season to taste and cook gently for 15 minutes.

Cook the pasta in boiling salted water, drain and stir in the cheese then the sauce. Serve at once.

1
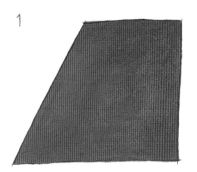

2

3

4

RAVIOLI STUFFED WITH ZUCCHINIS (COURGETTES) AND THEIR FLOWERS

Ravioli con ripieni di zucchini e fiore

PASTA

250 g (8 oz) spinach leaves
Salt
500 g (1 lb) white flour
4 eggs, 2 egg yolks

FILLING AND SAUCE

1 kg (2 lb) zucchinis (courgettes)
100 g (3½ oz) butter
10 zucchini (courgette) flowers
  (squash blossoms) (optional)
100 g (3½ oz) ricotta cheese
200 g (6½ oz) diced mozzarella
  cheese
Salt
Black pepper
50 g (1½ oz) freshly grated
  Parmesan cheese

THIS RECIPE COMES from Parma, famous for its cheese and ham. The ravioli looks effective with one sheet of green pasta covered by one of pale yellow.

Method: To make the pasta, wash the spinach leaves, then cook them quickly over a high heat, adding a pinch of salt. (The water clinging to the leaves will be sufficient.) Remove the spinach when it is limp but still bright green, drain well and plunge into cold water. When the spinach is cool, drain, squeeze out any remaining moisture, and purée.

Make the dough with half the flour and half the eggs. Add the spinach purée. Work into a smooth dough, knead for 10 minutes, then cover and leave for 10 minutes to rest, before rolling out as one large thin sheet. Make the white pasta in the usual way (see page 7) with the remaining eggs and flour. Roll out into another large thin sheet.

To make the sauce, choose two or three small zucchinis (courgettes), slice them finely and gently cook in the melted butter. If you are using flowers remove the stamens and pistils then add to the zucchini (courgette) slices. Cook for another 3 minutes.

To make the filling, roughly chop the remaining zucchinis (courgettes) and cook in boiling salted water. Drain, purée and then stir in the ricotta and mozzarella. Season to taste. Arrange this filling on the pasta sheet at regular intervals, cover with the second sheet, and cut out the ravioli measuring about 5 cm (2 in) square, sealing the edges well. When ready to eat, cook in boiling salted water until soft, lift out with a slotted spoon, and serve sprinkled with Parmesan and the sauce. Add a little black pepper and serve at once.

AUBERGINE (EGGPLANT) RAVIOLI

Ravioli di melanzane

PASTA

450 g (14½ oz) flour
3 eggs
a little water if the dough is too dry

FILLING

150 g (5 oz) ricotta cheese
2 aubergines (eggplants)
Salt
30 mL (2 tablespoons) olive oil
6 fresh basil leaves
Black pepper

300 mL (½ pt) fresh tomato sauce
    (see page 8)
50 g (1½ oz) freshly grated
    Parmesan cheese
6 sprigs fresh basil

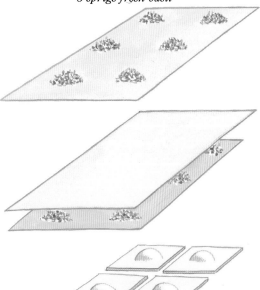

THIS IS AN ELEGANT version of the classic combination of pasta, aubergine (eggplant) and tomato. Do not drown the ravioli in too much tomato sauce or the dish loses its subtlety. The ravioli can be prepared as much as a day in advance. Sprinkle with semolina to keep them from sticking together and store in the refrigerator.

Method: Make the fresh pasta (see page 7).

To make the filling, drain the fresh ricotta in a sieve then put in a hot oven at 190°C (375°F) for about 15 minutes until it becomes hard (*infornata*). It can be bought already *infornata* in some specialty shops.
   Peel the aubergines (eggplants), cut them into rough wedges, sprinkle with salt and leave for an hour to purge the bitter juices. Rinse and dry, then fry in the heated oil until cooked. Put on paper towel to drain the excess oil and when cool purée with the ricotta and basil leaves. Season to taste.

To make the ravioli, roll out the pasta into two thin sheets and arrange spoonfuls of the filling at regular intervals. Cover with the second sheet of pasta and cut out square ravioli measuring about 5 cm (2 in), sealing the edges very firmly.
   When ready to serve, cook the ravioli in boiling, salted water and when they are ready lift out with a slotted spoon. (The cooking time will vary depending on the thickness of the pasta and the amount of filling.) Top each serving with a little tomato sauce, Parmesan cheese and a sprig of basil.

AGNOLOTTO WITH SPINACH AND CREAM

Agnolotto di spinaci alla crema

PASTA

300 g (9½ oz) flour
3 eggs

FILLING

100 g (3½ oz) ricotta cheese
100 g (3½ oz) cooked and drained
 spinach, puréed
60 g (2 oz) freshly grated
 Parmesan cheese
Salt
Black pepper
6 whole and unbroken egg yolks

SAUCE

200 g (6½ oz) cooked and drained
 spinach, puréed
50 mL (3⅓ tablespoons) fresh
 cream
Salt

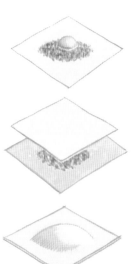

THE SMALL TOWN of Costigliole D'Asti, in Piedmont, attracts lovers of good food and wine from all over Italy. One of the great delights is the restaurant Guido, run by the Alciati family. Guido serves regional dishes to perfection and the Signora Lidia is an expert at creating new variations on a traditional theme. In this original recipe, each agnolotto is filled with spinach and one egg yolk. When the sumptuous white truffles are in season Guido adds a few flakes on top for the extra blissful touch. This is a feast for special occasions.

Method: Make the pasta (see page 7) and roll out 12 squares 10 cm (4 in) long.

You can cook, drain and purée the spinach for the filling and the sauce together. Use one-third of the puréed spinach for the filling and two-thirds for the sauce.

To make the filling, put the ricotta in a strainer and leave to drain for at least 30 minutes. Mix together the spinach, ricotta and Parmesan cheese. Season to taste. Spoon a little of this mixture on the middle of a square of pasta. Hollow out a small dimple in the middle of the spinach mixture and place an egg yolk in the hollow. Cover with another square of pasta, pressing on the edges to make sure the agnolotto is well sealed. Repeat to make another five agnolotti.

Make the sauce by mixing the spinach with the cream. Season to taste.

Cook the agnolotti in boiling salted water for about 2 minutes, then carefully remove with a slotted spoon. Spread a little sauce on each plate and carefully arrange an agnolotto on top.

TORTELLI WITH ASPARAGUS FILLING AND SAUCE

Tortelli agli asparagi

PASTA

450 g (15 oz) flour
3 eggs
A little water if the dough is
    too dry

ASPARAGUS FILLING

300 g (10 oz) green asparagus tips
    about 10 cm (4 in) long, saving
    the ends for the sauce
150 g (5 oz) drained ricotta cheese
75 g (2½ oz) freshly grated
    Parmesan cheese
50 mL (3⅓ tablespoons) fresh
    cream
Salt
Black pepper

ASPARAGUS SAUCE

The tender stalks of the asparagus
    (the tips of which are used for
    the filling)
100 g (3½ oz) butter, melted
Salt
Black pepper
50 g (1½ oz) freshly grated
    Parmesan cheese
12 asparagus tips (2 per person),
    for garnish

I REMEMBER EATING this elegant dish in Verona, where it was made with the tender locally grown green asparagus.

Method: Make the pasta (see page 7). Roll out the pasta into a thin sheet and cut fluted rounds of about 6 cm (2½ in) diameter.

To make the filling cook the asparagus tips quickly in boiling salted water. Purée the asparagus and mix to a paste with the ricotta cheese, Parmesan and cream. Season to taste. Keep in the refrigerator for at least 30 minutes to get firm. If the filling is still too liquid leave it to drain some more in a sieve.

Spoon some filling on the middle of a circle of pasta and cover with another circle of pasta, using a slight pressure to seal the edges together. When all the tortelli are made cover with a cloth and put in a cool place until ready to cook.

To make the sauce cook the asparagus stalks in boiling salted water and pass through a food mill. Stir in the melted butter and season to taste. Gently cook the remaining asparagus to garnish each plate of pasta.

Cook the pasta in boiling salted water and remove the tortelli with a slotted spoon when they are cooked. Serve into individual plates with the sauce, grated Parmesan and the whole asparagus tips.

RAVIOLI WITH ARTICHOKES
Ravioli ai carciofi

THIS IS ONE OF MY favourite pasta fillings which today can be enjoyed in many different Italian regions. In Rome it is served at Costanza, using an old family recipe, and in Liguria in Balzi Rossi.

Method: Make the pasta (see page 7). To make the filling, wash the artichokes and cook them in boiling salted water with the lemon. When they are cooked remove the tough leaves and 'choke' and slice the rest of the artichoke. Melt the butter and gently fry the leek until soft. Add the sliced artichokes to the leek for a few minutes to amalgamate the flavours. Then add the eggs, cheese and olive oil. Season to taste.

The ravioli will be about 5 cm (2 in) square so you need to roll out several long strips of pasta 5 cm (2 in) wide. Spoon the vegetable mixture on to the pasta strip at regular intervals. Cover with an identical strip of pasta and seal the long edges using the prongs of a floured fork. Now cut out individual squares and seal the remaining edges in the same way. (A pasta cutting wheel makes the process easier.) If possible, the ravioli should be arranged on a floured surface so that they do not touch and covered with a tea-towel. If you need to make them long in advance they should be covered with fine semolina to prevent them sticking together, loosely wrapped and stored in a refrigerator. When you are ready to cook them, shake off all the semolina.

Cook the ravioli in a large saucepan of boiling salted water. Drain and dress with melted butter and chopped thyme or oregano.

PASTA

500 g (1 lb) flour
4 eggs
2 egg yolks

ARTICHOKE FILLING

10 fresh artichokes
1 lemon, cut in half
50 g (1½ oz) butter
1 leek, sliced
3 hard-boiled eggs, sliced
75 g (2½ oz) freshly grated
    Parmesan cheese
30 mL (2 tablespoons) extra virgin
    olive oil
Salt
Black pepper

DRESSING

75 g (2½ oz) butter, melted
1 teaspoon chopped thyme or
    oregano

Onion Ravioli

Ravioli di cipolla

PASTA

300 g (9½ oz) flour
Salt
100 g (3½ oz) lard
30 mL (2 tablespoons) water

FILLING

50 mL (3⅓ tablespoons) extra
    virgin olive oil
500 g (1 lb) onions, thickly sliced
50 g (1½ oz) semolina
3 egg yolks
Salt
Black pepper
200 g (6½ oz) freshly grated
    pecorino cheese

ALTHOUGH SARDINIA'S CAGLIARI restaurant Dal Corsaro is more famous for its seasonal fish dishes, this unusual ravioli is one of its great triumphs. The pungent Sardinian pecorino cheese adds the final touch.

Method: The pasta is made in the usual way (see page 7) but lard and water are used instead of eggs and the dough needs to be kneaded for 10 minutes. Leave to rest for at least an hour before rolling out into 2 large thin sheets.

To make the filling, heat the oil, add the onion and when it turns golden brown, stir in the semolina and cook for another 5 minutes. Allow to cool then stir in the 3 egg yolks and season to taste.

Make the ravioli by arranging spoonfuls of the filling on one pasta sheet at regular intervals 4 cm (1½ in) apart. Cover with the second sheet, seal the edges and cut out the ravioli. When ready to serve cook in boiling salted water for 5 minutes, lift out with a slotted spoon and cover with lots of pecorino cheese and black pepper.

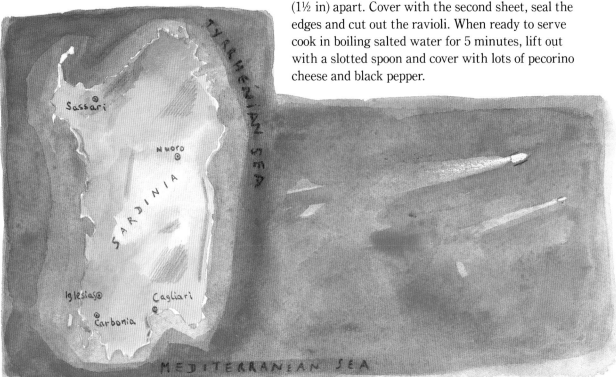

RAVIOLI WITH BORLOTTI (CRANBERRY) BEANS AND PARMESAN

Ravioli di borlotti e parmigiano

PASTA

450 g (14½ oz) flour
4 eggs

FILLING

400 g (12 oz) borlotti (cranberry)
    beans
Salt
45 mL (3 tablespoons) olive oil
1 clove garlic, minced
2 sprigs rosemary
150 g (5 oz) freshly grated
    Parmesan cheese
Black pepper
1 shallot (spring onion/scallion),
    finely sliced
1 tablespoon of rosemary blades
    removed from the sprig

IN THE PAST, BEANS were known as *la carne dei poveri*, or the poor man's meat. Today they are eaten with relish by rich and poor alike and this recipe shows just how good they can be.

Method: Make the pasta (see page 7).

Put the beans to cook in boiling salted water for about 30 minutes. Drain. If you are using dried beans leave them to soak overnight and increase the cooking time. The beans should be cooked until they are soft all the way through.

Heat half the oil and add the minced garlic and the rosemary. Remove from the heat as soon as the garlic begins to change colour and stir in the beans. Leave covered for 10 minutes for the flavour to be absorbed. Remove the rosemary and purée the beans and garlic with the Parmesan cheese. Season to taste.

Roll out the pasta into two thin sheets and arrange regular spoonfuls of filling on the bottom sheet. Cover with the second sheet of pasta and cut out square ravioli measuring about 5 cm (2 in). Seal the edges firmly.

When you are ready to eat, cook the ravioli in boiling salted water.

Heat the remaining oil and cook the shallot (spring onion/scallion) until soft. Add the blades of rosemary. Toss the drained ravioli in the oil and rosemary mixture. Serve at once.

PASTA FRITTERS
Frittelle di pasta

500 g (1 lb) angel's hair pasta
Salt
150 g (5 oz) freshly grated
    Parmesan cheese
75 g (2½ oz) butter, melted
30 g (1 oz) mushrooms (or ham),
    chopped and cooked
3 eggs
Black pepper
Oil for frying

THESE CRISP LITTLE pasta fritters make unusual nibbles to serve with drinks before dinner and you can use many different ingredients. They can even be made with leftover pasta, but are most effective made with very thin pasta.

Method: Cook the pasta in boiling salted water and drain. Stir in the cheese, melted butter and mushrooms. Beat the eggs with a little salt and pepper and stir into the mixture. Heat the oil until hot. With a fork make little tangles of pasta, about the size of a large walnut. Drop these little pasta balls into hot oil and fry until golden brown. Drain on paper towels and serve at once.

CRÊPES STUFFED WITH WATERCRESS IN SWEET PEPPER SAUCE

Crespelle al crescione con salsa di peperoni

CRÊPES

100 g (3½ oz) flour
2 eggs
125 mL (4½ fl oz) milk
125 mL (4½ fl oz) water
Salt
Black pepper
Butter for frying

SAUCE

3 sweet red peppers
60 mL (4 tablespoons) extra virgin
*   olive oil*
Salt

FILLING

500 g (1 lb) watercress
30 g (1 oz) butter
2 cloves garlic, finely chopped
100 g (3½ oz) ricotta cheese
75 g (2½ oz) freshly grated
*   Parmesan cheese*
Salt
Black pepper

THE SWEET PEPPER SAUCE in this recipe contrasts with the tart watercress to make a pleasingly different dinner party starter.

Method: Make six large or 12 small crêpes (see page 55) and leave them to cool.

To make the sauce, put the sweet peppers in a hot oven or under a hot grill for 10 minutes until the skin blisters. Peel off the skin and discard the seeds and tough fibres. Chop the peppers into rough pieces and cook in a little boiling water until they are soft. Drain and purée, adding the oil to make a smooth sauce. Add salt to taste.

To make the filling, remove the thick stalks from the watercress, wash, dry well and put to wilt in a pan with the butter and garlic. Process the watercress with the ricotta and Parmesan cheeses and season to taste.

Spread the crêpes with the filling, fold into four and arrange in a shallow buttered oven dish. Cover with sauce and cook at 180°C (350°F) for 10 minutes. Serve at once.

 # CRÊPES WITH RADICCHIO

Crespelle al radicchio

CRÊPES

100 g (3½ oz) flour
2 eggs
125 mL (4½ fl oz) milk
125 mL (4½ fl oz) water
Pinch of salt
Butter for frying

BECHAMEL SAUCE

50 g (1½ oz) butter
50 g (1½ oz) flour
1 L (1¾ pt) hot milk
Salt
Black pepper

FILLING

50 g (1½ oz) butter
2 shallots (spring onions/scallions),
*   finely chopped*
500 g (1 lb) radicchio, chopped
100 mL (3½ fl oz) white wine
Salt
Black pepper
12 steamed prawns (shrimp)
*   (optional), cut into small pieces*
30 g (1 oz) freshly grated
*   Parmesan cheese*

TREVISO IS THE TRADITIONAL home of radicchio but this elegant dish can be found gracing dinner plates in every region. The crêpes should be prepared in advance and allowed to cool so that they are easy to handle. The filling can also be prepared ahead of time and the actual *crespelle* assembled at the last moment. I often add a few steamed prawns (shrimp) to the filling to create a pleasing combination of sweet and bitter flavours.

Method: Make six crêpes (see page 55) and leave them to cool, separated with sheets of paper towel or foil.

To make the bechamel sauce, melt the butter and stir in the flour. Cook for 3 minutes then gradually add the hot milk. Simmer for about 10 minutes, stirring continuously, then season to taste.

To make the filling, melt the butter and cook the shallots (shallots onions/scallions) until soft. Add the radicchio and cook for 5 minutes. Add the wine, season to taste and cook for another 5 minutes.

Mix *half* the bechamel into the radicchio mixture. If you are using prawns add them to the mixture.

Spoon some filling into the middle of each crêpe and fold in half and half again to resemble a handkerchief. Put the crêpes into one long, shallow buttered oven dish or six individual dishes and cover with the remaining bechamel sauce. Sprinkle the cheese over the top and cook in an oven at 220°C (425°F) for 15 minutes.

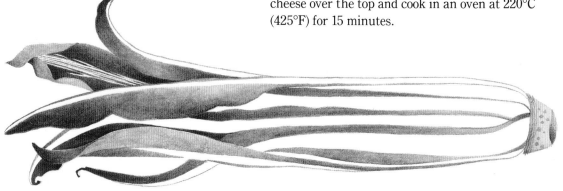

LITTLE 'SAILS' OR CRÊPES FROM THE AEOLIAN ISLANDS

Velette all' Eoliana

CRÊPES

100 g (3½ oz) flour
2 eggs
125 mL (4½ fl oz) milk
125 mL (4½ fl oz) water
Pinch of salt
Butter for frying

FILLING

250 g (8 oz) fresh mozzarella
*   cheese, diced*
500 mL (16 fl oz) fresh tomato
*   sauce (see page 8)*
150 g (5 oz) freshly grated
*   Parmesan cheese*
12 basil leaves
Black pepper

HOMER SPEAKS OF the islands off Sicily as the kingdom of Aeolus, the god of the winds. When Odysseus was on his way home to Ithaca after the Trojan war he landed here and, as a gift, Aeolus gave him the winds shut inside a bag, so that he would not be blown off course. This was a thoughtful gesture for the islands are very windy and the sea is often extremely rough. These little crêpe sails, served by the restaurant Filippino in Lipari, will help you steer your way through to a very successful dinner party. Either make 12 small crêpes or six larger pancakes.

Method: Make the crêpes in advance so that they are easy to handle. Beat all the ingredients together and let the batter stand at room temperature for a few hours. Heat the butter in a small pan and make 12 small crêpes of about 15 cm (6 in) or six larger ones. Stack them on a plate with a piece of foil between each one and allow to cool.

In the middle of each crêpe put some mozzarella and cover with a spoonful of tomato sauce and a little Parmesan cheese (save some Parmesan for later). Fold the crêpe in half and half again, and arrange in a greased oven dish with the corners pointing upwards like a sail. If you have six individual dishes you can make little 'boats'. Prepare all the crêpes in the same way then spoon over a little tomato sauce, Parmesan cheese, basil leaves and black pepper. Cook in an oven at 220°C (425°F) for 10-15 minutes.

CRÊPES WITH CHEESE AND BROAD (FAVA) BEANS

Crespelle di formaggio di fossa con purée di fave

CRÊPES

100 g (3½ oz) flour
2 eggs
125 mL (4½ fl oz) milk
125 mL (4½ fl oz) water
Pinch of salt
Butter for frying

SAUCE

30 g (1 oz) butter
2 shallots (spring onions/scallions),
· chopped
45 mL (3 tablespoons) dry white
wine
100 mL (3½ fl oz) light stock
500 g (1 lb) fresh broad (fava)
beans, shelled
Salt
Black pepper

FILLING

6 firm, ripe tomatoes, peeled,
seeded and diced
150 g (5 oz) cheese such as fontina
or Emmenthal, diced

IN ROMAGNA, NEAR Forli, there is a long tradition of maturing cheese made from ewe's milk in underground storage chambers dug out of the limestone. One theory is that this custom started when the local people hid grain and essential food supplies from the frequent raids of marauding Saracens. Others believe that these storage chambers were used to store snow to form ice houses. Today the cheese is put in the caves at the end of August, sealed in, and opened at the end of November, usually on St Catherine's day. This is the signal for great local celebrations. This recipe can be made equally successfully with other cheeses.

Method: Make six large or 12 small crêpes in advance (see page 55). Allow to cool.

To make the sauce, heat the butter and gently cook the shallots (spring onions/scallions), until soft. Pour in the wine, allow to evaporate then add the stock. Add the broad (fava) beans (the easiest way to shell the beans is to boil them for 5 minutes then pop off the outer skin), finish cooking until they are soft, then season to taste. Purée to make a dense sauce.

Butter an oven dish that will hold all of the rolled crêpes in one layer. Arrange some tomato and cheese in the middle of each crêpe, roll up and place in the dish with the seam side down. Brush with a little melted butter and cook in a 200°C (400°F) oven for 5 minutes.

To serve, heat the individual plates, spread each with a layer of hot bean sauce and arrange the crêpe on top. Serve at once.

SPINACH CRÊPES

Crespelle ai spinaci

CRÊPES

100 g (3½ oz) flour
2 eggs
125 mL (4½ fl oz) milk
125 mL (4½ fl oz) water
Salt
Butter for frying

FILLING

500 g (1 lb) washed spinach
1 egg, beaten
50 g (1½ oz) freshly grated
*   Parmesan cheese*
Nutmeg
Salt

50 g (1½ oz) butter
30 g (1 oz) freshly grated
*   Parmesan cheese*

WHEN SPINACH IS used to stuff pasta it is usually mixed with ricotta cheese. I like this recipe because the spinach taste is very definite, enhanced by the Parmesan cheese. The crêpes and filling can be prepared in advance and everything assembled ready to go in the oven. This makes it an easy dish to serve when you are entertaining.

Method: Make six large or 12 small crêpes (see page 55) and leave them to cool.

Cook the spinach in the water remaining on the leaves after washing and drain very well in a fine sieve, using the back of a wooden spoon to push out all the moisture. Stir in the beaten egg, 50 g (1½ oz) Parmesan cheese, and season to taste with nutmeg and salt. Fill the crêpes with this mixture and roll up to resemble cannelloni. Arrange in a single layer in an oven dish with the seam side down. Brush with melted butter and sprinkle with 30 g (1 oz) Parmesan and heat in a 180°C (350°F) oven for 15 minutes.

AUBERGINE (EGGPLANT) GNOCCHI

Gnocchi di melanzane

6 medium-sized aubergines
   (eggplants), peeled and cut into
   rough cubes
Oil for deep-frying
50 g (1½ oz) freshly grated
   Parmesan cheese
1 teaspoon oregano
6 basil leaves
80 g (3 oz) flour
2 egg yolks
Salt
Black pepper
Butter, fresh tomato sauce (see
   page 8), basil leaves and freshly
   grated Parmesan cheese for
   garnish

THESE DELICIOUS GNOCCHI can be served with
melted butter, Parmesan cheese, and just a delicate
touch of fresh tomato sauce and basil.

Method: Sprinkle the aubergine (eggplant) with salt
and leave to purge the bitter juices for at least 1 hour.
Rinse and pat dry.

Heat the oil then fry the aubergine (eggplant)
pieces until they are cooked but not crisp. Remove
with a slotted spoon and put to drain on paper
towels. Purée the aubergine (eggplant) with the
grated cheese, oregano and basil, then stir in the
flour and egg. Season to taste. Put the mixture in the
refrigerator for 1 or 2 hours.

When you are ready to cook the gnocchi, drop
spoonfuls of the mixture (or fill a forcing bag [pastry
bag] and pipe out ribbons of dough which can be cut
into 3 cm [1 in] lengths) into briskly boiling salted
water in a wide, shallow pan. The gnocchi are cooked
when they float to the surface. Remove them with a
slotted spoon to avoid breaking them. Garnish with a
little butter, a few spoonfuls of fresh tomato sauce,
basil leaves and freshly grated cheese.

PUMPKIN GNOCCHI
Gnocchi di Zucca

*1 kg (2 lb) fresh pumpkin, cut into
 large pieces*
250 g (8 oz) flour
*30 g (1 oz) freshly grated
 Parmesan cheese*
1 large egg
Salt
Black pepper
*Butter, Parmesan cheese and a
 little nutmeg, for garnish*

FERRARA IS FAMOUS for its fresh pasta filled with pumpkin. These light, delicate pumpkin balls make an interesting variation. For special occasions I like to buy a Cinderella-type pumpkin, carefully hollow it out, and bring the gnocchi to the table in the decorative pumpkin shell.

Method: Cook the pumpkin pieces for an hour in a 170°C (325°F) oven. When the pumpkin is cooked and fairly dry, remove any rind then purée. If the pulp seems too liquid, reduce it by boiling over a high flame. Use 450 g (14½ oz) of pulp and stir in the flour, cheese, egg and seasoning. Let the mixture stand in the refrigerator for at least half an hour.

In a wide, shallow pan bring water to a brisk boil, add salt and then drop in spoonfuls of the pumpkin mixture. (If you prefer, fill a forcing bag [pastry bag] with the mixture, pipe out ribbons of dough and cut them into 3 cm [1 in] lengths.) The gnocchi are cooked when they float to the surface. Remove quickly with a slotted spoon and serve at once, covered with melted butter, freshly grated Parmesan cheese and a little grated nutmeg.

SPINACH GNOCCHI WITH BEAN SAUCE

Gnocchi di spinaci con fagioli

GNOCCHI

400 g (12 oz) floury (baking)
potatoes
300 g (9½ oz) spinach leaves,
chopped
180 g (6 oz) flour
2 egg yolks
Pinch nutmeg
Salt

SAUCE

150 g (5 oz) dried haricot (navy)
beans, soaked for 12 hours
Salt
Black pepper
3 leeks, sliced into thin rings
100 g (3½ oz) butter
12 basil leaves

THIS IS AN INTERESTING, substantial dish which can be served as a tasty vegetarian treat.

Method: To make the gnocchi, cook the potatoes in their skins. Remove the skins while still hot and mash the potatoes. Boil the spinach leaves until wilted, drain very thoroughly and add the potatoes. Stir in the flour, egg yolks and seasoning. When the mixture is quite cool roll into thin cylinders, and cut into 2 cm (¾ in) lengths.

To make the sauce, drain the beans and cook until tender in boiling salted water. Melt half the butter and cook the leeks gently with a little salt and black pepper. When the leeks are soft add the basil leaves, cover and remove from the heat. Drain the beans and stir into the leeks. When ready to eat, cook the gnocchi in boiling salted water for about 3 minutes. When they float to the top, lift them out with a slotted spoon. Melt the remaining butter and pour over the gnocchi. Gently add the sauce and serve at once.

DRIED BEAN AND SEED STALL ·ROMA· 1992

ARTICHOKE GNOCCHI

Gnocchi ai carciofi

12 large artichokes
Salt
1 lemon, cut in halves
100 g (3½ oz) fresh breadcrumbs
100 g (3½ oz) flour
2 eggs
100 g (3½ oz) freshly grated
    Parmesan cheese
Black pepper
30 mL (2 tablespoons) extra virgin
    olive oil
1 small onion, finely chopped
1 tablespoon chopped mint
50 g (1½ oz) butter, melted

THESE LIGHT ARTICHOKE gnocchi are delicious, and I like to serve them surrounded by sliced artichokes and mint.

Method: Cook ten artichokes until tender in boiling salted water with half a lemon to prevent discolouring. When cool discard the tough outer leaves and choke to leave only the tender heart. Drain well then process with the breadcrumbs, flour, eggs and half the Parmesan. Season to taste. Leave the gnocchi mixture in the refrigerator for at least 30 minutes. When ready to cook, make small balls about the size of a walnut and arrange them on a plate so that they do not touch.

Cut the tips off the remaining two artichokes and ruthlessly strip off all the tough leaves until you get to the pale green. Rub with half a lemon and leave in a mixture of water and vinegar if you are not ready to use them immediately. When ready, drain, rinse and cut each into eight segments. Heat the oil and gently cook the onion until soft. Add the artichokes and cook for a few minutes. Season, add 2 tablespoons of boiling water and cover the pan. Cook gently for 10 minutes then add the mint and turn off the heat. While you are doing this, put the water for the gnocchi on to boil.

Drop the gnocchi into a large, shallow pan of boiling salted water. They are cooked as soon as they float on the top. Remove carefully with a slotted spoon because the gnocchi are very delicate. Arrange in a small pile on individual plates, covered with melted butter and the remaining cheese. Spoon the artichoke segments around the gnocchi and serve.

ROCKET GNOCCHI

Gnocchi di rughetta

1 kg (2 lb) floury (baking) potatoes
Salt
250 g (8 oz) flour
2 egg yolks
30 mL (2 tablespoons) extra virgin
*   olive oil*
1 small onion, finely chopped
1 clove garlic, finely chopped
150 g (5 oz) watercress
300 g (9½ oz) rocket leaves
Pepper

SAUCE

1 clove garlic, finely chopped
45 mL (3 tablespoons) extra virgin
*   olive oil*
200 g (6½ oz) rocket leaves
2 tomatoes, peeled and chopped
Salt
50 g (1½ oz) freshly grated
*   Parmesan cheese*

THIS IS ONE OF my favourite *rughetta* recipes, where the tangy herb is used in the gnocchi dough and repeated in the sauce. In Italy, floury potatoes are sold as 'potatoes for gnocchi'. You cannot make gnocchi with firm, waxy potatoes.

Method: To make the gnocchi, cook the potatoes in their skins in boiling salted water and while they are still warm peel and mash them by hand. (A processor spoils the consistency.) On a wooden board spread out the mashed potatoes and gradually work in the flour and the yolks. Heat the oil and gently brown the onion and garlic. Quickly cook the watercress and rocket in a little boiling salted water, drain and stir into the pan with the onions. Season to taste. Chop very finely in a food processor then work into the potato and flour dough. Form small balls the size of a walnut and allow to dry for 2 to 3 hours.

To make the sauce, cook the garlic in the oil, then add the rocket and tomatoes. Simmer for 5 minutes then season to taste.

When ready to eat, cook the gnocchi in boiling salted water. They are ready when they float to the top. Lift out with a slotted spoon and place in the pan with the sauce. Sprinkle with cheese and serve at once.

AUTUMN GNOCCHI

Gnocchi d' autunno

100 mL (3½ fl oz) light stock
300 g (9½ oz) beetroot, peeled and
cut into small pieces
500 g (1 lb) ricotta cheese, drained
5 eggs yolks
100 g (3½ oz) white flour
100 g (3½ oz) freshly grated
Parmesan cheese
Salt
Black pepper
100 g (3½ oz) pumpkin, boiled and
drained
50 g (1½ oz) melted butter

THE REDS AND oranges of autumn leaves are reflected in these colourful beetroot gnocchi, served in a pumpkin sauce.

Method: Boil half the stock, add the beetroot and cook until soft. Drain then purée in a food processor and add the ricotta cheese, yolks, flour, 80 g (2¾ oz) Parmesan, salt and pepper. Leave the mixture to cool then make the gnocchi using a spoon or pastry bag (see page 58).

Purée the pumpkin with the remaining stock to make smooth sauce.

Cook the gnocchi in boiling salted water and as they float to the surface remove carefully with a slotted spoon. Dress the drained gnocchi with the butter and remaining Parmesan and serve on a bed of pumpkin sauce.

VEGETABLES & SEAFOOD

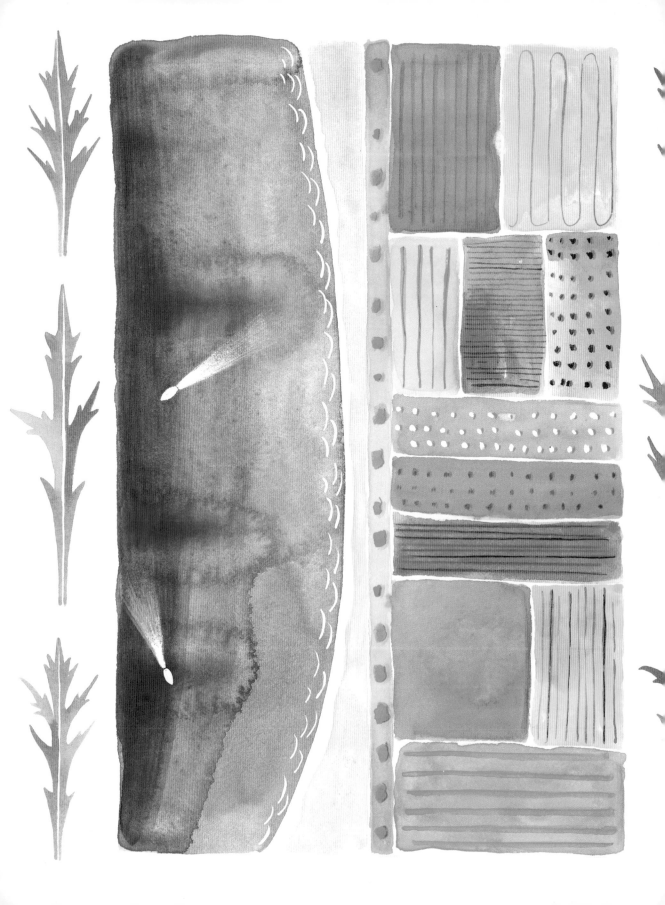

VEGETABLES & SEAFOOD

OUTSIDE ITALY, MANY restaurants create pasta dishes where
too many ingredients vie for attention, and the palate
becomes confused and dulled by the conflicting tastes.
Italian pasta relies on one or two perfect ingredients chosen
to interact with each other. Vegetables and seafood are often
combined in this very exciting way. Many of these recipes
are new but others use traditional partnerships in slightly
different ways. Although these recipes are served as starters
in Italy, many people will find that they have a complete,
balanced meal in one course if they increase the quantities.

TAGLIOLINI WITH TINY SQUID AND ROCKET

Tagliolini ai calamaretti e rughetta

30 g (1 oz) butter
15 mL (1 tablespoon) extra virgin
   olive oil
1 clove garlic, minced
1 red chilli pepper
300 g (9½ oz) wild rocket, washed
   and dried
600 g (1 lb 4 oz) very small squid,
   whole and cleaned
Salt
Pepper
600 g (1 lb 3½ oz) tagliolini

ROCKET USED TO BE grown round the statues of
Priapus, god of fertility, and the herb was believed to
be an aphrodisiac. The traditional *cucina povera* has
always made good use of the pungent flavour of the
wild variety. Today rocket enjoys new popularity all
over Italy and this combination of sharp, wild rocket
and small squid makes an exciting first course. If
wild rocket is not available substitute the milder
variety with the larger leaf, but in this case add the
rocket after the squid or you will lose the flavour.
This dish looks effective with small, tender squid
which are cleaned but left whole.

Method: Heat the butter and oil and add the minced
garlic and whole chilli. As the garlic begins to change
colour add the rocket leaves, and let them wilt very
quickly over a fierce heat. Now stir in the squid,
lower the heat, remove the chilli and season to taste.
   Cook the pasta in boiling salted water for a few
minutes, drain and stir quickly into the squid and
rocket. Serve at once.

TAGLIOLINI WITH CITRUS PEEL AND PRAWNS (SHRIMP)

Tagliolini con agrumi e gamberetti

3 lemons

3 oranges

100 mL (3½ fl oz) extra virgin olive oil

300 g (9½ oz) prawns (shrimp), shelled with central vein removed

Salt

600 g (1 lb 3½ oz) tagliolini

THE AMALFI COAST IS famous for its lovely lemons and oranges, and the restaurant Don Alfonso at Sant'Agata has made this light, delicate recipe from the good local ingredients.

Method: Remove the peel from the lemons and oranges, taking care to avoid the bitter white pith. Cut the peel into very fine julienne strips. The whole process can be done very successfully using a sharp zester. Heat the oil and gently cook the prawns (shrimp) for 3 minutes.

Fresh tagliolini will cook in a few minutes, and even the dry variety cooks quickly, so it is important to leave tagliolini only very briefly in briskly boiling salted water. Drain the pasta while it is still very much *al dente* and stir into the pan with the prawns (shrimp). Add the lemon and orange peel and serve at once.

TAGLIATELLE WITH PRAWNS (SHRIMP) AND CEPS

Tagliatelle mare e monte

300 g (9½oz) ceps
30 mL (2 tablespoons) extra virgin olive oil
1 clove garlic, crushed
Salt
Black pepper
3 ripe tomatoes, peeled, seeded and chopped
300 g (9½ oz) prawns (shrimp), shelled with central vein removed
45 mL (3 tablespoons) dry white wine
500 g (1 lb) tagliatelle
Chopped parsley, for garnish

THIS IS A DELICIOUS way of combining prized food from both the sea and the mountainside. You can make this with other types of mushrooms but the *funghi porcini* (ceps) add an extra dimension.

Method: Scrape the soil from the ceps and clean them with a damp sponge before slicing. It is important to dry them carefully so they do not become too wet and soggy. Heat half the oil and let the garlic get golden brown before discarding. Add the sliced ceps and cook gently for about 10 minutes. Season to taste then add the chopped tomatoes. Heat the remaining oil in another pan and quickly toss in the prawns (shrimp). Season. Cook for 1 minute then pour in the wine. Let the wine evaporate over a high heat then stir in the mushrooms and tomatoes. Cook the pasta in boiling salted water, drain, and stir in the sauce. Sprinkle with parsley and serve at once.

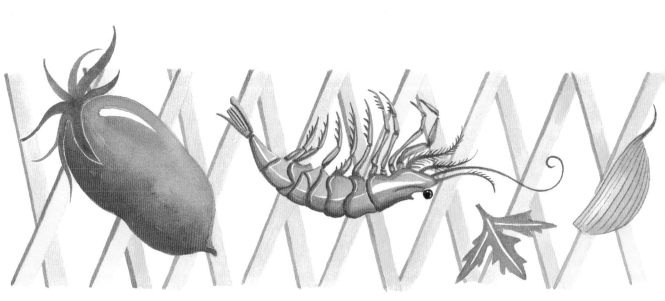

PARSLEY PASTA WITH FISH AND PESTO SAUCE

Stracci di prezzemolo e pesci al pesto

PASTA

75 g (2½ oz) parsley, finely chopped
5 eggs and 5 yolks
500 g (1 lb) flour
Salt

FISH

6 fillets of sole or red mullet
6 scallops, shelled
6 large prawns (shrimp) or scampi

PESTO

3 cloves garlic, peeled
40 g (1⅓ oz) pine nuts
50 g (1½ oz) freshly grated
  Parmesan cheese
400 g (12 oz) basil leaves
50 mL (3⅓ tablespoons) olive oil
Salt
Black pepper

THIS IS AN INTERESTING variation on the classic Ligurian dishes that combine pasta or fish with a basil sauce. The fresh pasta is made with parsley. A large quantity of egg is used to help the dough 'carry' the parsley. This recipe is intended as a first course but by increasing the quantity of fish and pesto sauce it can make a refreshing main course.

Method: To make the pasta, whisk together the parsley and eggs and add to the flour in the usual way to make a pasta dough (see page 7). Roll out the pasta and cut into rough diamond shapes about 5 cm (2 in) long.

To prepare the fish, cook the fillets, scallops and prawns (shrimp) in a steamer for 3 minutes.

Make the pesto by processing the garlic, nuts and cheese, then add the basil, processing until smooth. Season, then gradually add the oil with the processor running to make a thick, smooth mixture.

Cook the pasta in boiling salted water, drain, and stir in the pesto, using a little pasta water if necessary to make it mix in smoothly. Arrange the fish on top of the individual servings. Serve at once.

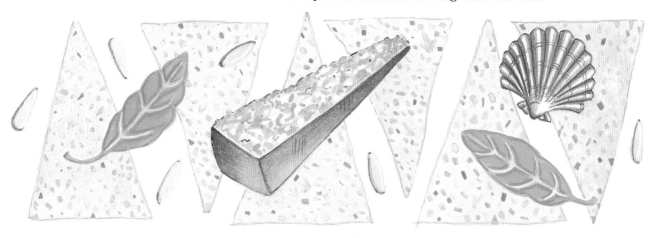

TAGLIOLINI WITH PRAWNS (SHRIMP) AND BASIL SAUCE

Tagliolini con gamberi e spuma di basilico

*500 g (1 lb) whole green prawns
(shrimp)*
*400 mL (13 fl oz) water for the
stock*
*1 shallot (spring onion/scallion),
chopped*
*100 g (3½ oz) fresh basil leaves,
roughly chopped*
*30 mL (2 tablespoons) extra virgin
olive oil*
50 g (1½ oz) butter
Salt
Black pepper
500 g (1 lb) green tagliolini

THIS IS A NEW recipe using the incomparable
Ligurian basil in a light, frothy sauce.

Method: Steam the prawns (shrimp) for a few
minutes then remove from their shells, reserving the
heads, and cut into three. Boil the water with the
chopped shallot and prawn (shrimp) heads and shells
for 15 minutes to make a stock then strain. Boil the
liquid once again over a high heat until the liquid has
reduced by half. Process the basil leaves with the
reduced stock, the oil and butter to make a thick,
smooth sauce. Season to taste. Cook the pasta in
boiling salted water, drain and stir in the prawns
(shrimp) and the basil sauce. Serve at once.

PENNE WITH PEAS AND RINGS OF CUTTLEFISH

Penne in bianco con le seppie e piselli

*35 mL (2⅓ tablespoons) extra
    virgin olive oil*
1 onion, sliced into fine rings
*400 g (12 oz) cuttlefish, main body
    only, sliced into thin rings*
100 mL (3½ fl oz) dry white wine
100 mL (3½ fl oz) light stock
Salt
Black pepper
1 clove garlic
250 g (8 oz) shelled peas
500 g (1 lb) penne
1 tablespoon chopped parsley

THE EXPRESSION *in bianco* — white — is used with pasta sauces to show that the ubiquitous tomato is omitted. Peas and cuttlefish are often served as a main course, but here the same pleasing combination is used very successfully with short pasta.

Method: Heat two-thirds of the oil and add the onion rings. When they soften add the cuttlefish. Pour in the wine and stock then season to taste. Cook gently until soft (usually about 20 minutes). Heat the remaining oil and brown the whole garlic clove. Remove the garlic, add the peas, season and gently cook the peas until just soft. Cook the pasta in boiling salted water, drain and stir in the cuttlefish, peas and parsley. Serve at once.

PENNE WITH ASPARAGUS AND RED MULLET

Penne con triglie e asparagi

400 g (12 oz) green asparagus
6 red mullet
100 g (3½ oz) butter
Salt
Black pepper
500 g (1 lb) penne

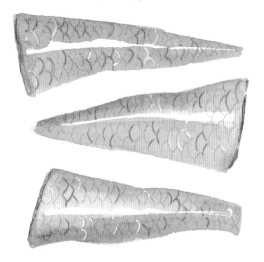

THE RED SKIN of the *triglie* looks very effective with the green asparagus, but any delicate white fish can be used if red mullet are not available.

Method: Cut the tips from the asparagus and keep to one side. Cut the tender parts of the stalks into 2 cm (¾ in) lengths. Leaving the skin intact (if using red mullet) fillet the fish, keeping six fillets whole and cutting the rest into thin strips. Melt a third of the butter and gently cook the whole fish fillets. After 5 minutes add the asparagus tips. Season to taste. Cook for a further few minutes until tender then cover and keep warm.

Melt half the remaining butter, cook the fish strips until done and season to taste. Cook the asparagus stalks in boiling salted water until tender, drain then add to the fish strips.

Cook the pasta in boiling salted water, drain and gently stir in the fish strips and asparagus stalks. Serve on a large heated plate with the whole fillets and asparagus tips arranged decoratively on top.

TAGLIOLINI WITH SHELLFISH AND SWEET PEPPERS

Tagliolini ai frutti di mare e peperoni

1 kg (2 lb) mixed mussels, clams
  and sea dates if available
Salt
75 mL (5 tablespoons) extra virgin
  olive oil
1 sweet yellow pepper, seeded and
  cut into fine strips
1 sweet red pepper, seeded and cut
  into fine strips
Black pepper
500 g (1 lb) tagliolini

THE COMBINATION OF sweet peppers and mixed shellfish makes this a memorable pasta. It can also be made equally successfully with dry pasta like linguine.

Method: Scrub and wash the shellfish well to remove grit. Discard any broken or open shells. Cover with lightly salted water and cook over a high heat until the shells open. Drain, reserve the cooking liquid to add to the pasta water and discard any closed shellfish. Remove the shellfish from their shells and keep warm.

In a large pan or wok heat the oil and cook the peppers for 10 minutes. Add the shellfish, 100 mL (3½ fl oz) of the shellfish cooking liquid and season to taste.

Cook the pasta in boiling salted water to which the remaining shellfish cooking water has been added. Drain and stir into the sauce. Simmer for another 2 minutes then serve at once.

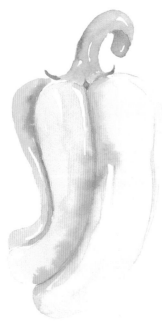

TAGLIATELLE WITH SCALLOPS AND FENNEL

Tagliatelle con capesante e finocchio

3 young, tender fennel bulbs, tough tubes and outer leaves removed, thinly sliced

60 mL (4 tablespoons) extra virgin olive oil

2 shallots (spring onions/scallions), finely chopped

12 or 18 scallops (2 or 3 per serving, depending on their size and how rich you want to make the dish), shelled, washed, dried and divided into quarters

150 mL (5 fl oz) dry white wine

Salt

Black pepper

2 cloves garlic, finely chopped

500 g (1 lb) tagliatelle

1 tablespoon chopped parsley

I FIRST ATE THIS interesting combination near Ravenna on the Adriatic coast where the scallops are small and tender.

Method: Steam the fennel slices until they are nearly soft.

Heat half the oil, add the shallots (spring onions/ scallions), and when they soften add the scallops. Cook for a few minutes then pour in the wine, reduce over a fierce heat and season to taste.

Heat the remaining oil in a large pan or wok, add garlic and as it begins to change colour add the steamed fennel slices and keep warm so the flavours mingle.

Cook the tagliatelle in boiling salted water, drain and stir into the pan with the fennel. Cook for another minute then check seasoning and stir in the parsley. Serve the pasta, arranging the scallops on top of each portion. Serve at once.

Large Snails Stuffed with White Fish and Radicchio

Lumaconi con ripieno di dentice e radicchio

1 small onion, roughly chopped
1 carrot, roughly chopped
1 celery stalk, roughly chopped
Salt
1 kg (2 lb) dentex, daurade or sea
   bream, cleaned
50 g (1½ oz) butter
500 g (1 lb) radicchio leaves, cut
   into thin strips
Black pepper
300 g (9½ oz) cream cheese or
   mascarpone
200 mL (7 fl oz) milk
500 g (1 lb) lumaconi
50 g (1½ oz) freshly grated
   Parmesan cheese

White fish and radicchio make an unusual filling for large dry pasta 'snails'. The pasta can be stuffed in advance and put in the oven to finish off just before you eat.

Method: Cook the onion, carrot and celery in boiling salted water then poach the fish on top of the vegetables for about 10 minutes. Remove the fish and strain and reserve the cooking liquid to add to the pasta water. Skin the fish and remove it from the bones.

Melt the butter, add the radicchio and cook gently until the leaves wilt. Season to taste. Purée the fish and stir in half the cream cheese and half the milk. Check the seasoning then gently fold in the radicchio.

Cook the pasta in boiling salted water, to which the fish stock has been added. When the pasta is pliable but not soft, drain. Using a teaspoon fill each 'snail' with the fish mixture and arrange in a lightly buttered shallow oven dish. Combine the remaining cream cheese with the rest of the milk, pour over the top of the pasta and sprinkle on the Parmesan. Cook in an oven at 250°C (500°F) until golden brown. Serve at once.

RADICCHIO TAGLIATELLE WITH PRAWNS (SHRIMP)

Tagliatelle di radicchio con gamberi

4 eggs
175 g (5¾ oz) fresh radicchio
    leaves, cut into fine ribbons
½ teaspoon salt
500 g (1 lb) semolina
30 mL (2 tablespoons) olive oil
1 clove garlic, finely chopped
300 g (9½ oz) shelled prawns
    (shrimp)
1 lemon
100 mL (3½ fl oz) dry white wine
Salt
Black pepper

IN ROME, IN Via Odescalchi 35, Cleto and Liliana Cellini produce an imaginative range of fresh pasta, gnocchi and crespelle, using seasonal vegetables in a myriad of ways. I find I always buy more than I planned because I can't resist all the tempting innovations. Their fresh pasta made with radicchio is very good. Following the Cellinis' advice I like to serve it with prawns and radicchio to complete the pleasure.

Method: Beat the eggs and stir in just over half the radicchio. Add the salt to the semolina and gradually work in the egg mixture, until you have a smooth dough. Knead energetically, using a food processor if preferred. Roll out a thin sheet of pasta, roll up, and cut into thin ribbons. Shake out the ribbons and arrange them in little piles. Allow to dry for 30 minutes.

Heat the oil, add the garlic and when it changes colour, stir in the prawns. Cook gently for 3 minutes then add the remaining radicchio leaves and cook until they wilt. Add a squeeze of lemon, the wine, and season to taste. Cook the pasta in boiling salted water, drain and stir in the prawn mixture.
Serve at once.

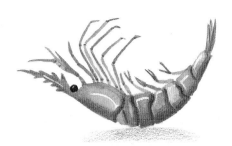

FUSILLI OR PENNE WITH MUSSELS AND POTATOES

Fusilli con cozze e patate

500 g (1 lb) mussels
Salt
250 g (8 oz) potatoes
100 mL (3½ fl oz) olive oil
500 g (1 lb) fusilli or penne
1 chilli pepper, whole
4 cloves garlic, finely chopped
1 tablespoon chopped parsley

IN THE SOUTH of Italy the combination of mussels and potatoes is often found in the *cucina povera*. In Puglia, there is a dish called *tiella* made with rice and mussels. It is a complete meal in itself. This variation is made with short pasta.

Method: Wash the mussels well to remove the grit under running water, then scrape clean, discarding any broken or open shells. Cover with lightly salted water and cook over a high heat until the shells open. Remove the mussels from the shells, discarding any that fail to open spontaneously, and strain and reserve the cooking liquid to add to the pasta water.

Peel the potatoes and boil in salted water until they are nearly cooked. They should not be allowed to get too soft. Cut into slices, then into sticks about 1 cm (⅓ in) wide. Heat half the oil and add the mussels and potatoes. Cook for 5 minutes and then add 3 tablespoons of the mussel liquid. Keep warm.

Cook the pasta in boiling salted water combined with the rest of the mussel liquid. Heat the remaining oil and cook the chilli pepper and garlic until golden brown. Discard the chilli. Drain the pasta and stir into the mussels and potatoes. Add the parsley, cook for a few minutes then pour on the garlic and oil. Serve at once.

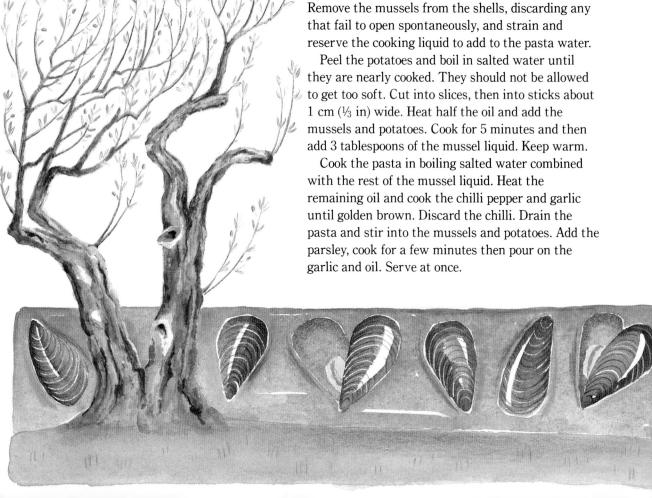

SPAGHETTI WITH ANCHOVIES AND ORANGE SAUCE

Spaghetti con acciughe in salsa di arancia

200 g (6½ oz) salted anchovies or
   canned anchovies, drained
30 mL (2 tablespoons) olive oil
1 clove garlic, finely chopped
2 oranges
1 tablespoon fresh breadcrumbs
50 mL (3¹/₃ tablespoons) orange
   liqueur such as Grand Marnier
Salt
500 g (1 lb) spaghetti
1 tablespoon chopped mint

IN CASTROVILLARI IN Calabria the restaurant Alia prepares new recipes with traditional ingredients. Oranges are often used with fish in Sicily but the combination, as in this recipe from Alia, is unusual for the mainland.

Method: If using salted anchovies, wash the salt out of the fish and remove the central bone. Cut the anchovies into pieces. Heat the oil and add the garlic. When the garlic begins to change colour add the anchovies and push with a wooden spoon until they 'melt' and form a thick cream. Remove the peel and white pith from the oranges and cut into little cubes. Add these orange cubes to the anchovies with the breadcrumbs and the liqueur. Add salt if necessary. Cook the pasta in boiling salted water, drain and stir in the sauce. Sprinkle with chopped mint and serve at once.

SPAGHETTI WITH TUNA AND LENTILS

Spaghetti al tonno e lenticchie

300 g (9½ oz) dried continental
   (green or brown) lentils
50 mL (3⅓ tablespoons) extra
   virgin olive oil
1 carrot, finely chopped
1 onion, finely chopped
1 stick celery, finely chopped
300 g (9½ oz) canned tuna,
   drained
1 tablespoon chopped parsley
Salt
Black pepper
500 g (1 lb) spaghetti

THIS HEALTHY, INEXPENSIVE pasta can be made from
the ingredients to be found in most store cupboards.
Tuna in olive oil makes a tastier sauce than tuna in
brine, and canned lentils can be used to save time.

Method: Soak the dried lentils in water for 5–6 hours,
then drain. Heat half the oil and add the vegetables
and the lentils. Add plenty of boiling salted water
and cook the lentils until soft — they usually take
about 25 minutes. Drain the lentils and mix them in
a bowl with the tuna, parsley, salt, pepper and
remaining oil. Cook the pasta in boiling salted water,
drain and stir in the sauce. Serve at once.

SPAGHETTI WITH BROCCOLI AND CLAMS

Spaghetti con broccolo romano e vongole

1 kg (2 lb) broccoli, divided into florets
Salt
30 mL (2 tablespoons) olive oil
5 cloves garlic, 1 chopped and 4 whole
2 chilli peppers
1 kg (2 lb) clams (or mussels) in their shells, scrubbed
150 mL (5 fl oz) dry white wine
1 tablespoon chopped parsley
500 g (1 lb) spaghetti

ROMANS ARE VERY FOND of their green cauliflower which has a stronger taste than the more usual white variety. I think the large-flowered broccoli makes a good alternative. This recipe works equally well with mussels in place of clams.

Method: Cook the broccoli in boiling salted water until half done. Drain and keep the broccoli water for the pasta.

Heat half the oil and add the chopped garlic clove and 1 whole chilli pepper. When they begin to change colour add the shellfish and turn up the heat. After a few minutes pour in the white wine and remove chilli. Remove the clams or mussels, reserving the cooking liquid, and take them out of their shells.

Heat the remaining oil and add the four whole garlic cloves and the other chilli pepper. When they begin to change colour, add the broccoli. Let the broccoli cook for a few minutes to absorb the flavours then discard the garlic and chilli pepper. Pour in the stock from the shellfish and cook for a few minutes. Add the parsley. Cook the pasta in the boiling broccoli liquid, adding more water if necessary. Drain and stir in the shellfish and broccoli. Serve at once.

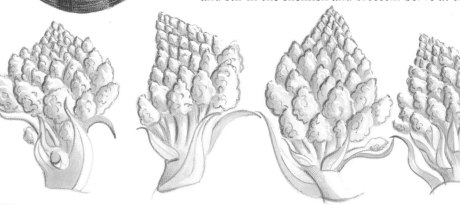

·MOSAIC· DESIGNS FROM PIAZZA ARMERINA· III-IV C.AD·

SEAFOOD

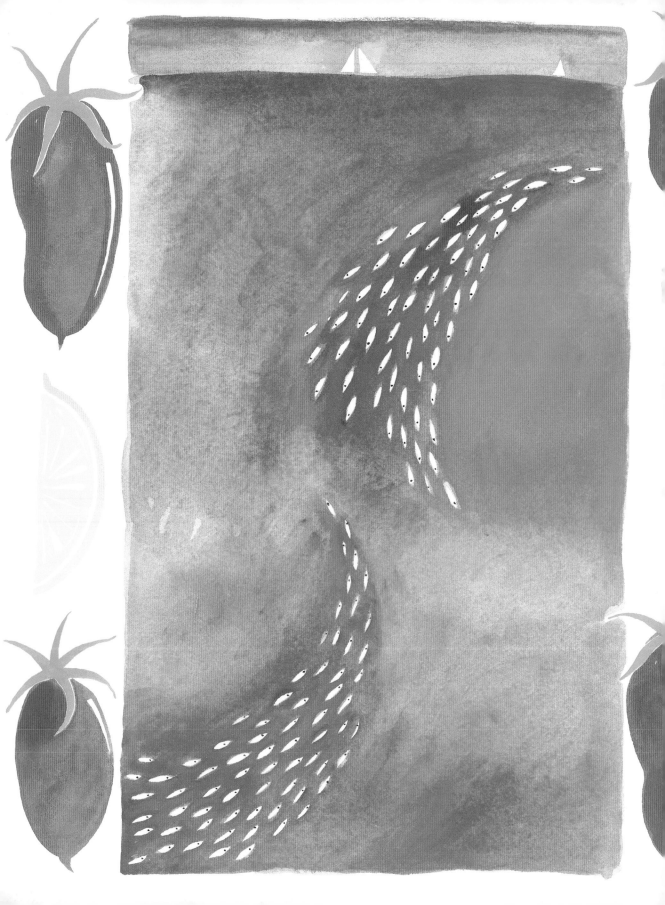

SEAFOOD

ITALIAN COOKING HAS ALWAYS relied heavily on good seafood from the Mediterranean, and some of the most delectable pasta recipes make masterly use of the sea's bounty. Lobster and swordfish are prized for their special flavour but the humble anchovy makes a great dish of pasta, and any white fish can be pounded to produce tasty fish balls that turn pasta into a complete meal.

In many cases it is difficult to find native Mediterranean fish outside Italy, but it is always possible to experiment for an acceptable substitute. I recommend Alan Davidson's book *Mediterranean Seafood*, to help you identify the fish you are seeking.

BUCATINI WITH FRESH TUNA SAUCE

Bucatini al ragù di tonno

*1 piece of tuna, weighing about
    1 kg (2 lb)*
3 cloves garlic, cut into slivers
12 sprigs fresh mint
*60 mL (4 tablespoons) extra virgin
    olive oil*
1 medium onion, finely chopped
*30 mL (2 tablespoons) tomato
    extract or concentrated tomato
    purée*
*50 mL (3⅓ tablespoons) dry white
    wine*
450 mL (14½ fl oz) boiling water
3 bay leaves
Pinch of ground cinnamon
Salt
Black pepper

THIS SICILIAN SPECIALITY is prepared beautifully in Palermo's L'Approdo restaurant where Gianni Botto uses the recipe perfected by his grandfather, Attilio Marchetto. Any long pasta can be used if you don't have bucatini but it is essential to use fresh tuna. This is one of the traditional recipes where the fish is cooked for the main course and the sauce from the fish is then used to dress the pasta. Today a little tuna is also served in flakes on top of the pasta. Also traditional is a very little matured caciocavallo cheese stirred into the sauce, usually about 1 tablespoon, but this strong cheese can ruin the delicate flavour if too much is used, so it is probably safer to omit.

Method: Wash and dry the tuna then make a series of deep incisions which you stuff with slivers of garlic and small sprigs of mint. Heat the oil until it is very hot then brown the tuna on all sides. Remove the tuna and in the same oil cook the onion until soft. Add the tomato extract and the white wine. Allow the wine to evaporate then pour on the boiling water and return the tuna to the pan. Add the bay leaves, cinnamon and seasoning and cook gently for 45 minutes. Remove the tuna from the sauce which should be very thick, and serve as a main course. (If desired a few flakes of tuna can be set aside to garnish the pasta later.)
    Cook the pasta in boiling salted water, drain and stir in the sauce. A ladle of pasta water can be added if the sauce is too dry.

LINGUINE WITH SWORDFISH

Linguine al pescespada

30 mL (2 tablespoons) olive oil
3 cloves garlic, crushed
5 ripe tomatoes, peeled, seeded and
    chopped
300 g (10 oz) swordfish
Salt
Black pepper
1 cup chopped fresh mint (or basil)
500 g (1 lb) linguine

SWORDFISH ARE A GREAT delicacy in Sicily. An eighteenth century English traveller describes the superstitious Sicilian fishermen using classical Greek as a charm to lure the fish to the boat. According to their lore the swordfish plunges into deep water and escapes if it overhears any Italian. Given the many existing recipes for swordfish I imagine the fish find the Sicilian dialect more acceptable!

Method: Heat the oil and gently cook the garlic. When it begins to change colour add the tomato and let the liquid evaporate. Cut the swordfish into small cubes. (In the past the trimmings from the cutlets to be grilled for the main course were often used for this recipe.) Add to the tomato and garlic. Season with salt and pepper and cook over a moderate heat for about 10 minutes. Add a little water if it seems too dry, and the mint. Cook the pasta in briskly boiling salted water. Drain and stir in the sauce. Serve at once.

SPAGHETTI WITH LOBSTER

Spaghetti all' aragosta

1 or 2 lobsters, weighing a total of 1.5 kg (3 lb)
50 g (1½ oz) butter
30 mL (2 tablespoons) olive oil
1 clove garlic, chopped
1 small onion, chopped
50 mL (3⅓ tablespoons) brandy
100 mL (3½ fl oz) dry white wine
1 tablespoon chopped parsley
1 kg (2 lb) very ripe tomatoes, peeled, seeded and cut into small cubes
Salt
Black pepper
500 g (1 lb) spaghetti

MY IDEA OF A perfect summer lunch is to sit on a terrace overlooking the sea with a glass of cool white wine from Friuli, and a plateful of this sumptuous pasta!

Method: Chop the lobster into small pieces, leaving the tail intact.

Heat half the butter and the oil and gently brown the garlic, onion and lobster. After a few minutes add the brandy and wine and allow to evaporate before adding the parsley and tomatoes. Season to taste and cook for about 20 minutes. Discard the lobster pieces but keep the tail warm. This will later be removed from the shell and served in thick slices on top of the pasta. Put the rest of the sauce through a fine food mill or strainer and keep warm.

Cook the pasta in boiling salted water and strain. Stir in the sauce and decorate with slices of lobster dressed with the remaining butter, melted. Serve at once.

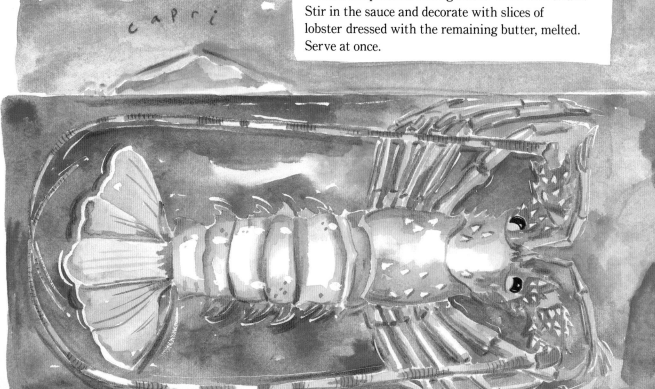

SANTE'S SHELLFISH SPAGHETTINI

Spaghetti alla Sante

45 mL (3 tablespoons) olive oil
4 cloves garlic
1 chilli pepper
*1 kg (2 lb) mixed fresh bivalves
(mussels, clams and other
bivalves like 'datteri',
'cannolicchi', 'telline',
'fasolare'), washed and scrubbed*
*300 g (9½ oz) little squid (about
5 cm [2 in] long if you can find
them), cleaned*
*300 g (9½ oz) prawns (shrimp),
cleaned*
100 mL (3½ fl oz) dry white wine
*300 mL (½ pt) fresh tomato sauce
(see page 8)*
Salt
500 g (1 lb) spaghettini

THIS RECIPE IS THE house specialty of the Florentine fish restaurant La Capannina di Sante. Sante Collesano is himself an experienced fisherman and he uses this expertise when he drives to the coast to choose the best of the catch at the great fish market at Porto Santo Stefano.

Method: In a very large pan (I use a wok) heat the oil and add the whole garlic cloves and chilli pepper. After 1 minute add the washed and scrubbed bivalves and cover the pan. As soon as the shells open add the cleaned squid and prawns (shrimp) and cook for 3 minutes. (If you are unable to find very tiny squid cut the sac into rings and the tentacles into small pieces.) Pour in the white wine and allow to evaporate, then add the tomato sauce. Heat the sauce through without allowing it to simmer. Remove the chilli and garlic and season to taste. Cook the pasta in boiling salted water for 3 minutes, drain and stir into the pan with the sauce so that it absorbs all the flavours as it finishes cooking. Serve at once.

SPAGHETTI WITH RED MULLET SAUCE

Spaghetti al sugo di triglia

45 mL (3 tablespoons) extra virgin
   olive oil
1 small onion, finely chopped
2 cloves garlic, chopped
1 tablespoon chopped parsley
600 g (1 lb 3½ oz) whole red
   mullets, filleted without
   removing the skin and the
   carcasses reserved for the stock
Salt
Black pepper
5 sprigs wild fennel or ferny leaves
   from fennel bulbs
25 pine nuts
25 sultanas
30 mL (2 tablespoons) dry white
   wine
4 ripe tomatoes, peeled, seeded and
   chopped
500 g (1 lb) spaghetti

THE ATTRACTIVE RED mullet has a delicate flavour
which is enjoyed all over the Mediterranean. In
Roman times the fish were highly prized and allowed
to grow to a great size. Today it is more common to
find the small variety (often about 10 cm [4 in] long
but they vary from 5 to 25 cm [2 to 10 in] in length).
I vividly remember my first encounter with these
tiny grilled fish when the rosy skin convinced me
that I was being served someone's pet goldfish!

Method: Heat one-third of the oil and gently brown
the onion, half the garlic and the parsley. Add the
fish carcasses and after a few minutes add 150 mL
(5 fl oz) boiling water. Season and stew for
15 minutes. Strain and reserve stock.

Heat the remaining oil, and add the fennel and
remaining garlic. When they begin to change colour
add the nuts and sultanas and, after a few minutes,
the fillets of fish. When they have absorbed the
flavours pour in the wine and turn up the heat so
that the wine evaporates. Now add the tomatoes and
the strained fish stock. Cook gently for 10 minutes.

Cook the spaghetti in boiling salted water, taking
care not to overcook. Drain and stir in the sauce.
Serve at once.

I usually remove the fish fillets from the sauce
with a slotted spoon before I stir the sauce and
spaghetti together because the fillets break easily. I
then spoon them into the serving bowl on top of the
spaghetti and sauce.

TAGLIATELLE WITH SCORPION FISH

Tagliatelle allo scorfano

30 mL (2 tablespoons) olive oil
3 cloves garlic, minced
1 kg (2 lb) ripe tomatoes, peeled
    and seeded
1 or 2 scorpion fish weighing a
    total 1 kg (2 lb), scaled and
    gutted
50 mL (3⅓ tablespoons) dry white
    wine
Salt
Black pepper
500 g (1 lb) tagliatelle
Chopped parsley or basil for
    decoration

IN ITALY THERE IS an expression 'ugly as a *scorfano*', but beauty is indeed in the eye of the beholder, as the proverb says, because my eyes light up whenever I sight one of these orange fish with their big head, bulbous eyes and lugubrious expression. In France it is called *rascasse* and is the prime ingredient in the majestic *bouillabaisse*, and most Mediterranean fish soups owe their inimitable flavour to the *scorfano*. In this recipe from the Marche region on the Adriatic coast the same ingredient makes a memorable pasta feast.

Method: Heat the oil, add the garlic and let it turn golden brown before adding the tomatoes. Cook for a few minutes then add the fish. Pour over the wine, season to taste, cover and cook slowly for about 20 minutes, adding a little water if it becomes necessary. Remove the fish and when it cools slightly remove from the bone and divide into pieces about 4 cm (1½ in) long. Cook the pasta in boiling salted water, drain and stir into the sauce. Serve with the pieces of fish and chopped parsley or basil on top.

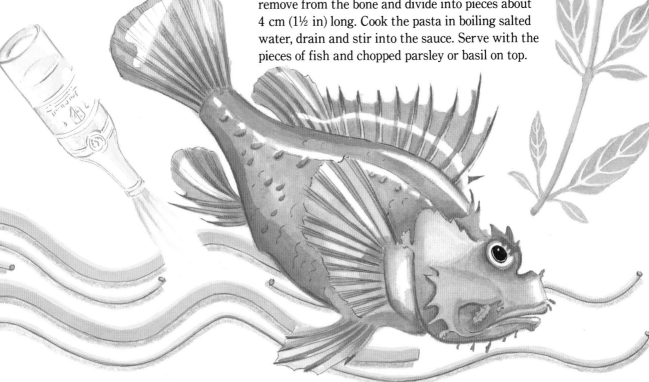

SPAGHETTI WITH SEA URCHIN SAUCE

Spaghetti con ricci di mare

50 sea urchins

50 mL (3⅓ tablespoons) extra
    virgin olive oil

20 mL (1⅓ tablespoons) lemon
    juice

Salt

Black pepper

500 g (1 lb) spaghetti

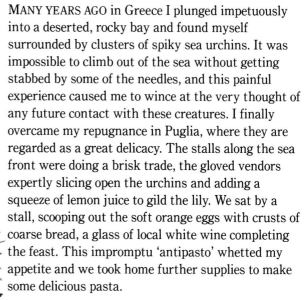

MANY YEARS AGO in Greece I plunged impetuously into a deserted, rocky bay and found myself surrounded by clusters of spiky sea urchins. It was impossible to climb out of the sea without getting stabbed by some of the needles, and this painful experience caused me to wince at the very thought of any future contact with these creatures. I finally overcame my repugnance in Puglia, where they are regarded as a great delicacy. The stalls along the sea front were doing a brisk trade, the gloved vendors expertly slicing open the urchins and adding a squeeze of lemon juice to gild the lily. We sat by a stall, scooping out the soft orange eggs with crusts of coarse bread, a glass of local white wine completing the feast. This impromptu 'antipasto' whetted my appetite and we took home further supplies to make some delicious pasta.

Method: Using heavy, protective gloves cut the sea urchins in half, like a grapefruit, and scrape out the orange cream. Place in a bowl and stir in the oil and lemon juice. Season to taste. Cook the pasta in boiling salted water, drain and stir in the sauce. Serve at once.

TAGLIATELLE WITH SCALLOPS

Tagliatelle con capesante

100 g (3½ oz) butter
1 leek, finely sliced
Salt
Black pepper
300 g (9½ oz) scallops, shelled
100 mL (3½ fl oz) dry white wine
400 g (12 oz) green tagliatelle

THIS DELICATE PASTA dish combines the green pasta from Emilia with the tender scallops from Romagna's Adriatic coast.

Method: Melt half the butter and gently cook the leek, adding a little water if it gets too dry. Season to taste. Melt the remaining butter and cook the scallops (whole if they are very small, but cut into two or three pieces if large) for 3 minutes, adding the white wine and seasoning. Add the scallops and their cooking liquid to the leek and let stand while the pasta is cooking so that the flavours amalgamate. Cook the tagliatelle in boiling salted water, drain and stir in the sauce. Add more black pepper and serve at once.

SPAGHETTI WITH DRIED FISH ROE

Spaghetti con la bottarga

75 g (2½ oz) bottarga *(dried fish roe)*
20 mL (1⅓ tablespoons) olive oil
2 cloves garlic, minced
Parsley, finely chopped
500 g (1 lb) spaghetti

THE MOST DELICATE *bottarga* comes from the grey mullet. The eggs are removed intact in their membrane then salted, pressed and dried in the sun. In Sicily and Sardinia the *bottarga* is made from tuna roe and the salami-like oblong is preserved in a wax casing. The tuna *bottarga* has a stronger taste than the mullet version and can best be savoured with a plate of pasta. It is advisable to cook the pasta in unsalted water to mitigate the salt in the fish roe. The best *bottarga* is a light rose colour.

Method: If the *bottarga* is dry remove the skin and grate. Crumble it into the olive oil. If it is still moist it will almost melt. Add the garlic and a generous amount of parsley and stir well to make a dense, creamy sauce. Cook the pasta in briskly boiling *unsalted* water, drain and stir in the sauce. A ladle of pasta water can be added if necessary to help coat every strand of pasta with the sauce.

BLACK TRENETTE WITH PRAWNS (SHRIMP)

Trenette al nero di seppie con gamberetti

30 mL (2 tablespoons) olive oil
1 clove garlic, crushed
500 g (1 lb) prawns (shrimp),
*   shelled and patted dry*
Salt
Black pepper
50 mL (3¹/₃ tablespoons) dry white
*   wine*
Ink sac from a cuttlefish, intact
1 tablespoon chopped parsley
250 g (8 oz) trenette

THE INK SAC FROM cuttlefish can be used to tinge dry pasta a glistening black which looks spectacular with pink prawns (shrimp) and green parsley. This dish is usually served in small portions as a starter. Double the quantities if you want normal-sized helpings.

Method: Heat the oil and add the crushed garlic. When it begins to change colour it should be discarded. Stir the prawns (shrimp) in the hot oil for 2–3 minutes, season and pour over the wine. After 1 minute remove the prawns (shrimp) and turn up the heat to let the sauce reduce then remove from the heat and stir in the contents of the ink sac and the chopped parsley. Cook the trenette in boiling salted water, drain, and stir in the sauce, letting it coat every strand of pasta. Add the prawns (shrimp) and serve at once.

TRENETTE WITH MUSSELS AND SAFFRON

Trenette alle cozze e zafferano

1 kg (2 lb) mussels
100 mL (3½ fl oz) dry white wine
30 mL (2 tablespoons) olive oil
2 cloves garlic, chopped
1 tablespoon chopped parsley
1 tablespoon chopped mint
Salt
Black pepper
500 g (1 lb) trenette
Saffron threads

INSTEAD OF THE saffron being dissolved, in this recipe the saffron stamens are added just before serving so that the rich aroma can be fully enjoyed.

Method: Scrub the mussels, discarding any which are cracked or remain open when touched, remove the 'beard', and put in a pan with the wine and a little water over a high heat. When the mussels have opened, take them out of the pan and remove them from their shells. Pour the cooking liquid through a fine strainer to remove any grit, and reserve.

Heat the oil, add the garlic and let it begin to change colour. Adding the mussels, parsley and mint. After a few minutes pour in the mussel liquid and turn up the heat to reduce and thicken the sauce. Season to taste. Cook the pasta in boiling salted water, drain and stir in the mussels. Put a pinch of saffron threads on top of each serving so the full flavour can be savoured.

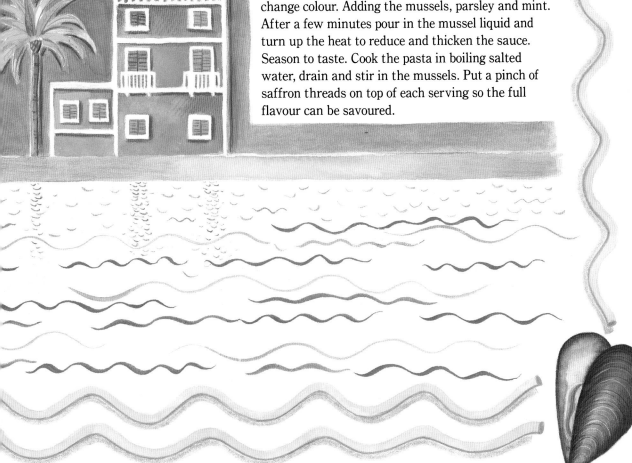

RIGATONI STUFFED WITH FISH

Rigatoni ripieni

300 g (9½ oz) fish fillets
60 mL (4 tablespoons) olive oil
Juice of 1 lemon
2 cloves garlic, minced
2 carrots, finely chopped
1 medium onion, finely chopped
1 tablespoon finely chopped parsley
Salt
500 g (1 lb) rigatoni
15 mL (1 tablespoon) olive oil
30 g (1 oz) breadcrumbs
500 mL (16 fl oz) fresh tomato
    sauce (see page 8)
50 g (1½ oz) freshly grated
    caciocavallo, pecorino dolce or
    other available cheese
Black pepper

IN SICILY THIS recipe is prepared with fresh sardines or fresh anchovies but any readily available, inexpensive fish can be substituted.

Method: Cover the fish fillets with oil, lemon juice, garlic, carrot, onion, parsley and salt and leave for at least 2 hours. Drain off the liquid and process the solids to form a dense cream.

Cook the pasta in boiling salted water until pliable, not soft, drain and fill with the fish mixture, using a pastry bag. Lightly oil a large oven dish, arrange the rigatoni and cover with breadcrumbs. Pour on the tomato sauce, sprinkle with grated cheese and pepper, then cook in an oven at 200°C (400°F) until golden brown. Serve at once.

LINGUINE WITH FISH BALLS

Linguine con polpette di pesce

100 g (3½ oz) stale white bread
  with crusts removed
Milk to soak bread
Fish fillets weighing about
  700 g (1½ lb)
2 eggs, separated
50 g (1½ oz) butter, melted
100 g (3½ oz) freshly grated
  Parmesan cheese
Salt
Black pepper
45 mL (3 tablespoons) olive oil
1 onion, finely chopped
300 g (9½ oz) ripe plum tomatoes,
  peeled and seeded
500 g (1 lb) linguine

THIS IS A FISHY VERSION of the old standby, spaghetti and meat balls. It is usually made with pike or other coarse lake fish but any firm-fleshed fish can be used.

Method: Soak the bread in a little milk to soften, then squeeze out the excess milk. Put the fish, egg yolks, melted butter, cheese and bread in a food processor and blend to a smooth paste. Add salt and pepper. Whip the egg whites until stiff and gently fold into the fish paste. Shape into little balls about the size of a walnut. Heat the oil, gently cook the onion then add the tomatoes. Squash the tomatoes with a wooden spoon then gently drop in the fish balls and allow to simmer gently for about 15 minutes until cooked.

Cook the pasta in boiling salted water, drain and stir in the sauce and fish balls. Serve at once.

SPAGHETTI WITH CRAB MEAT AND SAFFRON

Spaghetti con polpa di granchio

45 mL (3 tablespoons) extra virgin
   olive oil
250 g (8 oz) crab meat
50 mL (3⅓ tablespoons) dry white
   wine
Salt
Black pepper
A pinch of saffron, powder or
   filaments
400 g (12 oz) spaghetti
1 tablespoon chopped parsley

THIS PASTA CAN be prepared with any crab meat.
The saffron adds an intriguing touch of colour.

Method: Heat the oil and gently warm the crab meat.
If you are using fresh crab, cook for 10 minutes. Pour
in the white wine and season to taste. Dissolve the
saffron in a little warm water and stir into the pan
so that the crab meat takes on a golden hue. Cook the
pasta in boiling salted water, drain and stir in the
crab sauce and a little chopped parsley. Serve at once.

SPAGHETTI WITH RAW SALMON

Spaghetti con salmone crudo

500 g (1 lb) fresh salmon, skinned, boned and cut into small cubes
45 mL (3 tablespoons) lemon juice
60 mL (4 tablespoons) dry white wine
60 mL (4 tablespoons) extra virgin olive oil
2 teaspoons chopped wild fennel or dill
Salt
Black pepper
1 clove garlic
500 g (1 lb) spaghetti

IN THE LAST TEN years or so the Italians have developed a passion for the alien salmon and it appears on the table in many guises. This recipe is light and interesting, and it is often served cold in the summer months.

Method: Put the salmon in a bowl and cover with the lemon juice, wine, half the oil, the herbs and seasoning. Leave to marinate for at least an hour. When ready to serve heat the remaining oil, add the garlic clove and when it turns a golden brown remove it from the pan and discard. Cook the pasta in boiling salted water, drain and stir into the warm garlic oil. Drain the salmon, keeping some of the marinade to dress the pasta if it seems too dry. Stir in the salmon and serve at once.

If serving cold, the pasta must be plunged into cold water after being cooked, drained again then stirred into the cooled, aromatic garlic oil. The salmon is added just before serving.

FETTUCCINE WITH SPIDER CRAB

Fettuccine alla gran'seola

6 spider crabs
1 celery stalk
1 carrot
1 lemon, cut in half
45 mL (3 tablespoons) extra virgin
    olive oil
2 cloves garlic, chopped
1 chilli pepper, chopped
250 g (8 oz) tomatoes, peeled,
    seeded and chopped
500 g (1 lb) fettuccine
Salt
2 tablespoons chopped parsley

VENICE IS THE traditional home of a multitude of dishes served with this decorative crab. But in the outskirts of Viterbo, an Egyptian-born chef, Amin Ibrahim, has a specialty where the pasta is served spilling out of the crab shell as if it were an eccentric pink cornucopia. Ibrahim is master chef at the Aquilanti restaurant which has been in the Aquilanti family for three generations.

Method: Put the crabs, celery, carrot and lemon into a large pan and cover with cold water. Bring to the boil, cook for about 10 minutes then allow to cool. Remove the crabs and take the meat from the shells, being careful to save the whole upper body shell from each crab. Strain the cooking water and reserve. Heat the oil, add the garlic and chilli and when they start to change colour, add the crab meat. After 1 minute add the tomatoes and a little of the cooking water to make a thick sauce. Cook the pasta in boiling salted water and the remaining cooking liquid, drain and stir in the sauce and the parsley. With a large fork place a coil of pasta in each cleaned upper shell and arrange on individual plates with the pasta spilling out of the shell.

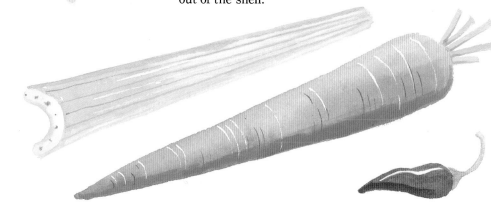

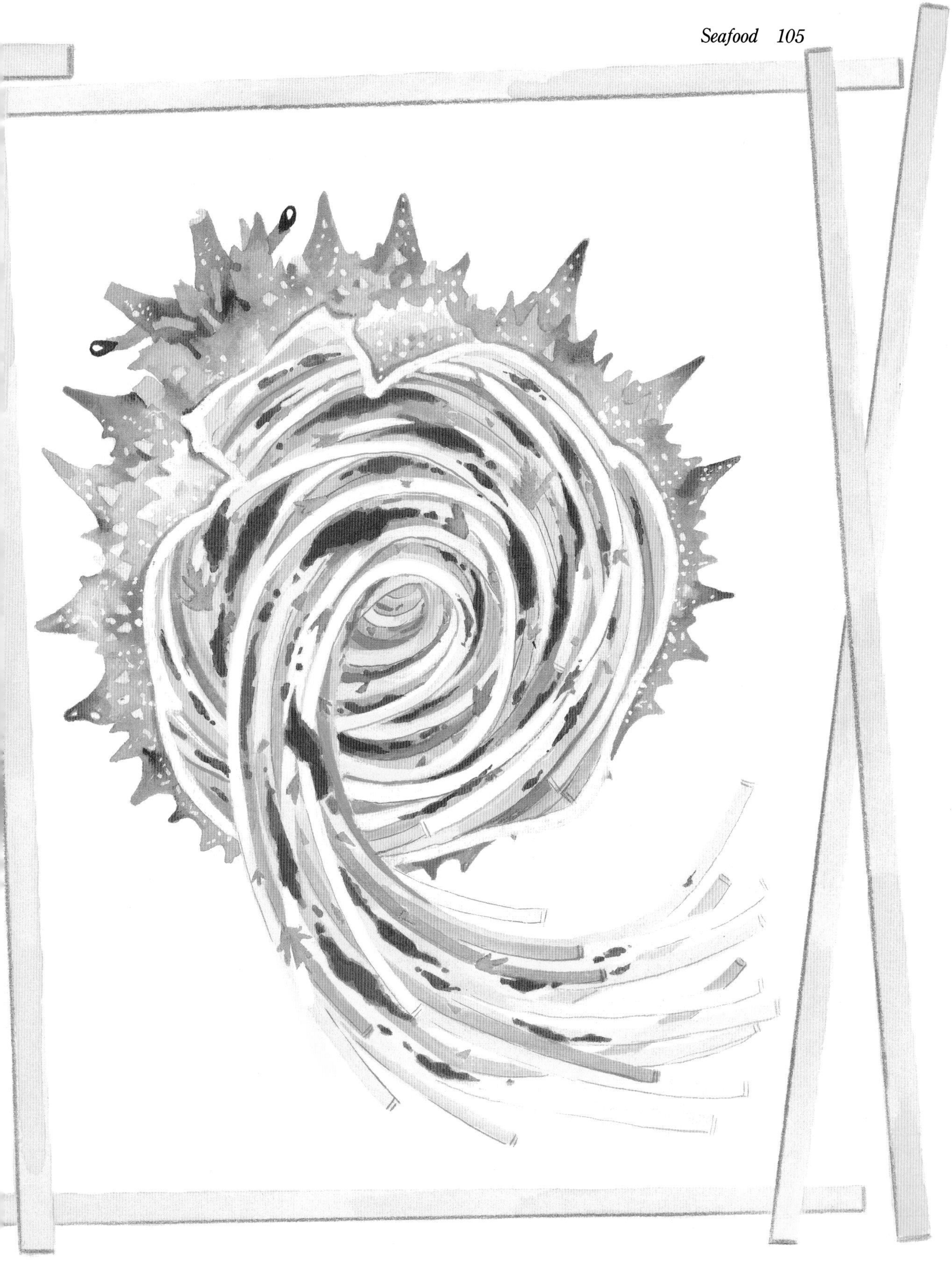

PENNE WITH TROUT FILLETS

Penne ai filetti di trota

Salt
Pepper
Flour, to coat the trout
6 small trout fillets
45 mL (3 tablespoons) extra virgin
  olive oil
2 cloves garlic, chopped
½ tablespoon rosemary blades
  removed from the sprig
1 tablespoon chopped parsley
50 mL (3⅓ tablespoons) dry white
  wine
500 g (1 lb) penne or other short
  pasta
15 mL (1 tablespoon) lemon juice
Thin threads of lemon peel, for
  decoration

ITALIAN COOKING USES rosemary to add a pungent note to trout dishes. I sometimes feel this flavour is too strong for fish freshly caught from a sparkling mountain stream, but it works wonderfully well with farmed trout.

Method: Season and flour the trout fillets then cut into pieces about 3 cm (1 in) long. Heat the oil, add the garlic and when it starts to change colour, add the trout, rosemary and parsley. Cook the fish lightly on both sides then pour in the wine. Cook for a few more minutes then remove from heat and keep warm.

Cook the pasta in boiling salted water, drain and stir in the lemon juice. With a wooden spoon gently add the fish sauce, taking care not to break up the fish. Serve at once, decorated with strands of lemon peel.

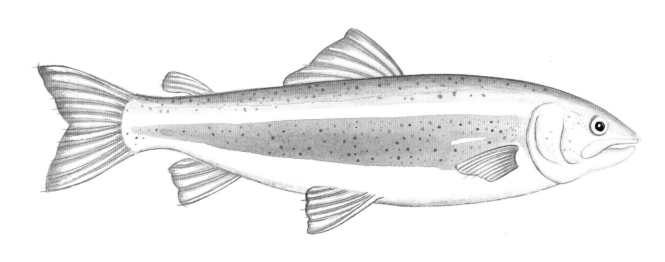

LINGUINE WITH EEL

Linguine con anguilla

Salt
300 g (9½ oz) skinned eel, cut into
*   small cutlets*
45 mL (3 tablespoons) olive oil
3 cloves garlic, chopped
1 chilli pepper, chopped
500 g (1 lb) linguine
50 g (1½ oz) parsley, chopped

IN UMBRIA THE EELS from the many lakes are used in a variety of recipes, and they make very good pasta sauces.

Method: Salt the pieces of eel then undercook them on the grill. The eel should be nearly opaque but not brown. Remove the bone and cut the flesh into small cubes.

Heat the oil, add the garlic and chilli pepper and when they begin to change colour add the eel. Cook very gently for 5 minutes so that the eel absorbs all the flavours.

Cook the pasta in boiling salted water, drain and stir into the fish sauce. Add the parsley, stir well and serve at once.

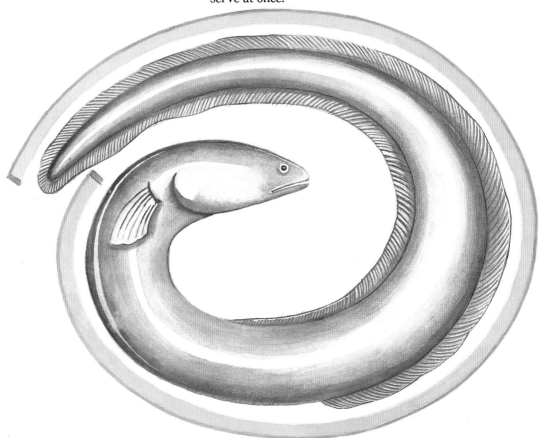

PASTA WITH ANCHOVIES

Pasta cu sardi a mari

12 anchovy fillets in oil
3 cloves garlic, chopped
2 tablespoons chopped parsley
45 mL (3 tablespoons) olive oil
Salt
Black pepper
100 g (3½ oz) breadcrumbs
500 g (1 lb) spaghetti
25 g (1 oz) pine nuts, lightly
   toasted
25 g (1 oz) sultanas, lightly toasted

THIS RECIPE COMES from Franca Colonna Romano's book *Sicilia in Bocca e nel Cuore*. Franca cares passionately about her island's traditional *cucina povera*, of which this recipe is a part. She explains that in Sicilian this dish is ironically called 'pasta with the sardines at sea' because it is made with canned anchovies which leaves the sardines still swimming in the sea.

Method: Remove the anchovy fillets from their oil, break them up and stir in a few drops of water to make a smooth paste. Add the garlic, parsley and two-thirds of the oil, stir and season to taste.

Heat a heavy pan and lightly toast the breadcrumbs before adding the remaining oil in a fine thread.

Cook the pasta in boiling salted water, drain and stir in the anchovy sauce. If the pasta seems too dry a little of the pasta cooking water can be added to the sauce. Decorate the individual servings with sprinklings of breadcrumbs, pine nuts and sultanas.

SALT DRYING. SICILY.

LINGUINE WITH SARDINES

Linguine alla salsa di sarde

45 mL (3 tablespoons) extra virgin
  olive oil
2 cloves garlic, chopped
8 canned sardines in oil, drained,
  boned and chopped
5 canned anchovy fillets, drained,
  boned and chopped
Juice of 2 lemons
Salt
Black pepper
500 g (1 lb) linguine
1 tablespoon chopped parsley

THIS IS A VERY quick and easy recipe that can be made with not much more than a couple of cans from the pantry!

Method: Heat the oil, add the garlic and when it begins to change colour add the sardines and anchovies. Cook gently until the sardines and anchovies 'melt' and you have a thick paste. Stir in the lemon juice and check seasoning. Cook the pasta in boiling salted water, drain and stir in the sauce. Sprinkle with parsley and serve at once.

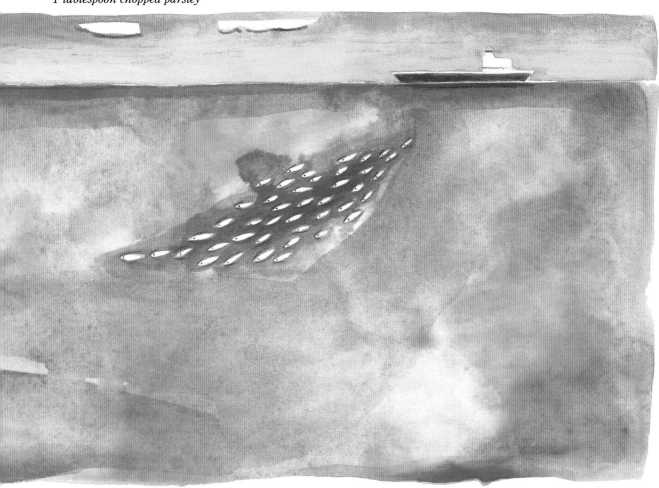

LASAGNE WITH SHELLFISH

Lasagne ai frutti di mare

PASTA

400 g (12 oz) flour
4 eggs

FILLING

30 mL (2 tablespoons) olive oil
1 onion, finely chopped
300 g (9½ oz) shelled scallops
50 mL (3⅓ tablespoons) brandy
Salt
Black pepper
300 g (9½ oz) shelled prawns
    (shrimp)
800 g (1¾ lb) shelled mussels

BECHAMEL SAUCE

75 g (2½ oz) butter
150 g (5 oz) flour
750 mL (1⅓ pt) milk
750 mL (1⅓ pt) fish or vegetable
    stock
1 cup fresh chopped basil or parsley
Salt
Black pepper

NOW THAT PEOPLE are eating less meat, the traditional lasagne seems to have lost its appeal. This lighter version makes an elegant first course for a dinner party since it can be prepared in advance, and cooked in the oven just before you eat. In Italy this is cooked in a very large shallow oven dish so that there are four layers of pasta and three of shellfish. I think it is better to use two or three smaller dishes if necessary, rather than increase the number of layers.

Method: Make the pasta (see page 7).

To make the filling, heat the oil and gently cook the finely chopped onion. Remove two-thirds of the onion and add the scallops to the pan remaining third. Cook for a few minutes, pour in one-third of the brandy, season to taste and cook until the brandy evaporates. Remove from the pan, wipe out the pan and repeat the procedure with half the remaining onion and brandy and the prawns (shrimp). Do the same thing with the mussels and the last of the onion and brandy.

To make the bechamel, melt the butter in a heavy pan and stir in the flour. Cook gently for 5 minutes then gradually stir in the milk and stock to make a thin bechamel sauce. Process the sauce with the basil or parsley to get a delicate green, perfumed sauce. Season to taste.

Roll out the pasta and cut four sheets the same size as your rectangular oven dish. If you are using smaller dishes cut four sheets for every dish. Cook the pasta sheets one at a time for a few minutes in boiling salted water and put on tea-towels to drain.

Grease the oven dish and cover with a sheet of pasta. Spread a little bechamel sauce over the pasta and then arrange the scallops in a single layer. Cover with the second sheet of pasta, spread over more bechamel sauce and arrange the mussels in a single layer. Cover with the third sheet of pasta another layer of sauce, then the prawns (shrimp). Put the last sheet of pasta on top, spoon over the remaining sauce and bake in an oven at 200°C (400°F) for 20 minutes. Serve at once.

SHELLFISH CRÊPES WITH PESTO SAUCE

Crespelle di frutti di mare al pesto

CRÊPES

100 g (3½ oz) flour
2 eggs
125 mL (4½ fl oz) milk
125 mL (4½ fl oz) water
Pinch of salt
Butter for frying

PESTO

1 clove garlic
30 g (1 oz) pine nuts
30 g (1 oz) Parmesan cheese
60 g (2 oz) fresh basil leaves
Salt
Black pepper
200 mL (7 fl oz) extra virgin
  olive oil

THIS SPECTACULAR DISH from Liguria makes a lovely first course for a dinner party. The crêpes and filling can be prepared in advance and assembled just before your guests are due to arrive. Even the pesto can be made in advance if you are prepared to ignore or discard the top layer which will have changed colour and become rather dark.

Method: To make the crêpes beat all the ingredients together and let the batter stand at room temperature for a few hours. Heat the butter in a small pan and make 12 small crêpes about 15 cm (6 in) diameter. Stack on a plate with a piece of foil between each crêpe and allow to cool.

To make the pesto, process the garlic, nuts and cheese, then add the basil and process until smooth. Season to taste then gradually add the oil with the processor running to make a thick, smooth mixture.

FILLING

15 mL (1 tablespoon) olive oil
25 g (¾ oz) butter
1 carrot, chopped
1 stick celery, chopped
1 clove garlic, chopped
1 small onion, chopped
500 g (1 lb) mixed shellfish
    (prawns/shrimp, scallops,
    mussels etc.)
10 mL (2 teaspoons) acquavita or
    brandy
Salt
Black pepper
1 egg
20 g (¾ oz) butter
½ tablespoon each of chopped dill,
    parsley and tarragon
24 long chives
50 g (1½ oz) melted butter

To make the filling, heat the oil and butter and gently cook the chopped vegetables until soft. Add the shellfish, cook for about 5 minutes, then pour over the acquavita and allow to evaporate. Season to taste. When the filling is cool, purée with the egg, butter and herbs.

Spoon some filling into the middle of each pancake then roll it up. Tie a chive loosely around each end so that the pancake looks like a wrapped sweet or candy. Arrange with the seam downwards in a single layer on a flat, rectangular, buttered oven dish.

Pour the melted butter over the pancakes and brown in a hot oven at 190°C (375°F) for about 5 minutes. Remove the dish from the oven and spread a generous spoonful of pesto sauce over the middle of each pancake parcel. Return to the oven for 2 minutes to warm the pesto, then serve.

POULTRY,
MEAT & HAM

POULTRY, MEAT & HAM

IN THE PAST, WHEN Italy was a comparatively poor country,
most people could not afford to eat meat very often, and
pasta was often served with the sauce or gravy from a piece
of meat that would be saved to provide another meal. Today
with the improved standard of living this is no longer the
case but it is still not very common to find pasta cooked with
meat or poultry. The modern trend is to use vegetables
and/or fish with pasta, and to serve the meat as a second
course. The recipes in this section include some of the more
interesting exceptions to the rule.

SPAGHETTI WITH DUCK SAUCE

Bigoli co l' anara

1 young duck, cleaned, with giblets
    reserved and finely chopped
1 onion, chopped
1 carrot, chopped
1 stick celery, chopped
Salt
Black pepper
45 mL (3 tablespoons) olive oil
50 g (1½ oz) butter
2 sage leaves
2 bay leaves
2 tablespoons of pomegranate juice,
    if available
500 g (1 lb) bigoli *or spaghetti*
100 g (3½ oz) freshly grated
    Parmesan cheese

IN THE VENETO region they make long, spaghetti-like pasta with buckwheat or wholewheat flour. These *bigoli* can be made quite easily with two eggs to every 500 g (1 lb) flour but you need a press or mincer with 4 mm (⅙ in) holes to get the uniform size. Spaghetti can be used in place of *bigoli*. Traditionally the sauce is made with the duck giblets while the pasta is cooked in the duck stock and the duck is served separately as a main course. If you prefer you can reserve the duck breast for another meal and use the darker meat for the sauce in place of the giblets.

Method: Put the duck to cook in a large pan of water (enough to cover) with the onion, carrot, celery and seasoning. If the duck is young and tender you will probably need to cook it for about 45 minutes. Remove the duck when tender and keep the stock to cook the pasta.

Heat the oil and butter and gently brown the duck giblets with the sage and bay leaves. Add the pomegranate juice halfway through the cooking when the ingredients have taken colour. If you are substituting duck meat for the giblets, pull the flesh from the bones and cut into small pieces. Put these in the pan of oil and herbs to absorb flavour.

Cook the pasta in boiling duck stock, adding more water if necessary. Drain, and stir in the sauce and the cheese. Serve at once.

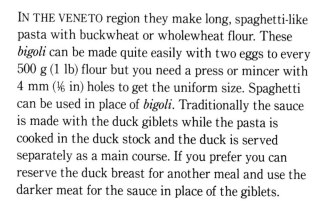

COMPOSITE OF DETAILS FROM ETRUSCAN "TOMB

PENNE WITH DUCK AND ORANGE

Penne al ragù di anitra e arancia

*1 duck weighing just under
    1 kg (2 lb)*
Salt
Black pepper
1 onion, peeled
45 mL (3 tablespoons) olive oil
2 cloves garlic, chopped
1 stick celery, chopped
1 carrot, chopped
2 bay leaves
*50 mL (3⅓ tablespoons) dry white
    wine*
Light stock
*Juice of 2 oranges (blood oranges if
    available)*
*Peel of 2 oranges, grated into thin
    threads*
500 g (1 lb) penne
50 g (1½ oz) butter, melted

THIS SUMPTUOUS new dish makes a great dinner
party first course.

Method: Rub salt and pepper over the duck and put
the peeled onion inside the carcass. Heat the oil and
gently brown the garlic, celery and carrot before
adding the duck and bay leaves. Pour in the wine and
enough stock to keep the duck and its drippings
moist. Cover and cook gently over a low heat for 45
minutes to 1 hour. When cooked, reserve the liquid
and remove the meat from the bones and cut into
small pieces. Pour the cooking liquid through a
strainer and add the orange juice, thin threads of
orange peel and meat.

Cook the pasta in boiling salted water, drain, and
stir in the melted butter and sauce. Serve at once.

FETTUCCINE WITH CHICKEN AND SWEET PEPPERS

Fettuccine con pollo alla Romana

*3 sweet peppers, red, yellow and
    green*
30 mL (2 tablespoons) olive oil
1 onion, chopped
2 cloves garlic, chopped
*1 chicken, boned and cut into
    small pieces*
*30 mL (2 tablespoons) dry white
    wine*
*15 mL (1 tablespoon) concentrated
    tomato paste*
100 mL (3½ fl oz) light stock
Salt
Black pepper
500 g (1 lb) fettuccine

ROME IS FAMOUS for its savoury chicken and sweet pepper casserole and this recipe uses the same winning combination in a robust pasta dish which can make a one-dish meal if desired.

Method: Roast the peppers over a high flame so that the skin blisters and can be easily removed. You can omit this step but peeling does make the peppers more digestible. Cut the peppers into strips.

Heat the oil and gently brown the chopped onion and garlic. Add the chicken pieces and brown them on all sides. Pour in the wine and the tomato paste diluted with a little light stock. Add the peppers and cook slowly to obtain a thick sauce. Add a little more stock if the sauce becomes too dry. Season to taste.

Cook the pasta in boiling salted water, drain, and stir in the sauce. Serve at once.

ROMAN MOSAIC . THIRD CENTURY AD

TAGLIATELLE WITH GUINEA-FOWL

Tagliatelle al ragù di faraona

60 mL (4 tablespoons) olive oil
1 large onion, finely sliced
1 stick celery, finely sliced
1 boned guinea-fowl weighing just
    over 1 kg (2 lb), chopped into
    small pieces
Salt
Black pepper
25 g (1 oz/2 tablespoons) flour
100 mL (3½ fl oz) dry white wine
200 g (7 oz) red tomatoes, peeled,
    seeded and chopped
1 sprig rosemary
1 tablespoon chopped parsley
500 g (1 lb) tagliatelle
100 g (3½ oz) freshly grated
    Parmesan cheese

THERE ARE COMPARATIVELY few pasta dishes using poultry but the Veneto region has some tasty traditional recipes which can make perfect one-dish meals for lunch or supper, or opulent starters for a more formal dinner.

Method: Heat the oil and gently cook the onion and celery. Season the guinea-fowl and add to the pan, browning the pieces on all sides. When they are nicely browned, sprinkle in the flour and stir with a wooden spoon until the flour has become golden brown. Pour in the wine and allow it to evaporate before stirring in the tomatoes and herbs. Cook gently for 15 minutes. Remove the rosemary.

Cook the pasta in boiling salted water, drain, and stir in the guinea-fowl sauce. Then stir in the cheese and serve at once.

FETTUCCINE WITH CHICKEN LIVER

Pappardelle con fegatini di pollo

100 g (3½ oz) butter
1 clove garlic, finely chopped
200 g (6½ oz) cleaned chicken
  livers, diced
4 sage leaves, finely chopped
1 sprig rosemary, finely chopped
Salt
Pepper
500 g (1 lb) fettuccine
75 g (2½ oz) freshly grated
  Parmesan cheese

IN TUSCANY, LIVER is prepared as it is for this recipe, spread on *crostini* (small savoury toasts) and served at the beginning of a meal. In this recipe the same combination of chicken livers and herbs is used to make a tasty, filling pasta dish. Although it is traditionally made with wide ribbons of pappardelle, I prefer to use the thinner fettuccine.

Method: Heat the butter and add the garlic. When it begins to change colour add the liver and herbs. Season to taste and cook gently until tender.

Cook the pasta in boiling salted water, drain, and toss in the cheese before stirring in the sauce. Serve at once.

CERAMIC DESIGN FROM PUGLIA. 20TH. C.

PENNE WITH CALF'S LIVER MOUSSE

Penne alla spuma di fegato

50 g (1½ oz) butter
1 small onion, chopped
1 clove garlic, chopped
200 g (6½ oz) calf's liver, roughly
  chopped
2 bay leaves
Salt
Black pepper
50 mL (3⅓ tablespoons) dry
  Marsala wine
1 tablespoon chopped parsley
100 mL (3½ fl oz) cream
500 g (1 lb) penne
50 g (1½ oz) freshly grated
  Parmesan cheese (optional)

DRY MARSALA WITH its muted sweet note adds an extra dimension to this rich pasta. It is worth trying to find the right wine but if this proves impossible try using a medium dry sherry. I prefer this dish without cheese but Parmesan can be served separately if desired.

Method: Melt the butter and gently fry the chopped onion and garlic until they begin to change colour. Add the liver and bay leaves and season to taste. Cook for about 5 minutes then pour in the Marsala. Cook for another few minutes then remove the bay leaves and process the liver with the chopped parsley to make a smooth creamy sauce. Quickly blend in the cream.

Cook the pasta in boiling salted water, drain and stir in the sauce. Serve at once.

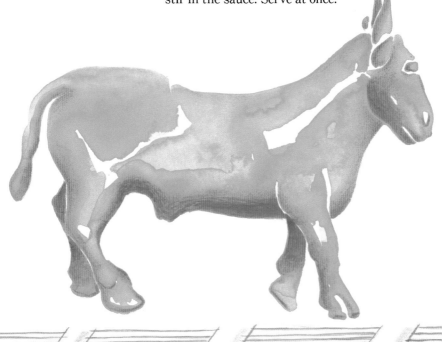

ETRUSCAN   BRONZE   OX.   FOURTH C. B.C

PAPPARDELLE WITH WILD BOAR
Pappardelle al cinghiale

15 mL (1 tablespoon) olive oil
1 onion, minced
1 carrot, chopped
2 slices streaky bacon, chopped
200 g (6½ oz) lean wild boar,
  chopped
200 g (6½ oz) cleaned and sliced
  fresh mushrooms, or 50 g
  (1½ oz) dried mushrooms
100 mL (3½ fl oz) dry red wine
100 mL (3½ fl oz) grappa, brandy
  or acquavita
Salt
Pepper
500 g (1 lb) pappardelle
100 g (3½ oz) freshly grated
  Parmesan cheese
25 g (1 oz) butter, melted

WILD BOAR USED TO be hunted in the woods of Umbria and Tuscany and their succulent meat was used to enrich many traditional meals. Today these splendid, robust dishes are becoming rarer. The fierce animals roam freely in protected conservation areas and farmed 'wild' boar are available. In the absence of *cinghiale* this recipe can be prepared with ham or pork.

Method: Heat the oil and gently brown the onion, carrot, bacon and meat. If you are using dried mushrooms, soak them in a little tepid water for 20 minutes before using. When the onion is a golden brown add the sliced mushrooms and cook for 2–3 minutes. Turn up the heat and pour in the wine and grappa. When the liquid is very much reduced, cover the pan and cook slowly for another 25 minutes. Season to taste. Cook the pasta in boiling salted water, drain, and stir in the cheese, melted butter and sauce. Serve at once.

DETAIL OF ETRUSCAN VASE

ORECCHIETTE WITH LAMB SAUCE

Orecchiette al sugo di agnello

30 mL (2 tablespoons) olive oil
100 g (3½ oz) butter
Spikes from 1 sprig of rosemary
1 kg (2 lb) lamb, boned and cut
   into small pieces
Salt
Black pepper
500 g (1 lb) orecchiette or short
   concave pasta
75 g (2½ oz) freshly grated
   Parmesan cheese

THESE LITTLE EAR-SHAPED flour and water pasta are a specialty of Puglia in the south. The 'heel' of Italy was colonised by the Greeks whose influence can be seen in the dialect spoken in some localities, *griko*, and in the local cooking where lamb predominates. Lamb is usually roasted on a spit and the stuffed intestine, known by a variety of ribald names, is regarded as a great delicacy. This recipe, however, is in the *cucina povera* tradition where the meat sauce is used to enrich the pasta and the meat is served for another meal. Today some people would use both meat and gravy to dress the pasta.

Method: Heat the oil and butter, add the rosemary, and brown the pieces of meat on all sides. Season to taste, cover and cook slowly until tender adding a little water from time to time. Do not add too much water because the sauce should be thick. When the meat is cooked, put it aside until you are ready to serve the pasta.

Cook the pasta in boiling salted water, drain and serve the sauce and some of the meat if you want a more sustaining dish. The freshly grated Parmesan is served separately.

6TH C. AD SHEEP DESIGN

TAGLIOLINI WITH ROAST VEAL JUICES

Tagliolini con la bagnabrusca

*1 piece of roasting veal, about 1 kg
(2 lb)*
2 cloves garlic, cut into slivers
1 sprig rosemary
Salt
Black pepper
45 mL (3 tablespoons) olive oil
*50 mL (3⅓ tablespoons) dry white
wine*
Light stock
1 egg
Juice of 1 lemon
500 g (1 lb) tagliolini

MANY REGIONS IN ITALY have enlarged their traditional cuisine by adopting and absorbing Jewish recipes from the old ghettos. This simple, delicious recipe has not been 'discovered' by many gentiles, but I find it very good. The meat is usually served at a separate meal, often the day before.

Method: With a sharp, pointed knife make deep incisions in the veal and spike it with slivers of garlic and spikes of rosemary and season. Roast in the oil, sprinkling with wine and stock from time to time so that the meat drippings form a thick sauce. Do not let the roasting pan become dry. When the meat is cooked to your liking, strain the cooking juices. Make the sauce by beating the egg and lemon juice together. Add this to the cooled cooking juices. Heat this sauce in a double saucepan to avoid curdling.

Cook the pasta in boiling salted water. Drain and stir in the sauce. Since this is a kosher recipe, cheese is not usually served with this dish.

SAN GIORGIO MAGGIORE VENICE. 1992

BAKED GREEN TAGLIOLINI WITH HAM

Tagliolini verdi gratinati al prosciutto

50 g (1½ oz) butter
25 g (1 oz/2 tablespoons) flour
200 mL (7 fl oz) hot milk
100 g (3½ oz) butter
150 g (5 oz) lean ham, preferably
  prosciutto crudo, *cut into little*
  strips
500 g (1 lb) tagliolini verdi
Salt
Black pepper
150 g (5 oz) freshly grated
  Parmesan cheese

ALTHOUGH THE GRITTI PALACE always offers several traditional Venetian dishes on their menu, this delicate green pasta is one of their chef's specialities and it is a universal favourite.

Method: To make the sauce, melt the butter, stir in the flour and cook for 3 minutes. Gradually add the hot milk, stirring until thick and smooth then simmer for another 10 minutes.

Melt three-quarters of the butter in a pan and cook the ham. Cook the tagliolini for 2 minutes in boiling salted water, drain and stir in the ham and about half the sauce. Season to taste and transfer into one large shallow ovenproof dish or six individual dishes. Cover the top with the remaining sauce, dot with butter, then cover thickly with the freshly grated Parmesan cheese.

Brown under a very hot grill or put in a 220°C (425°F) oven until a golden brown. Serve at once.

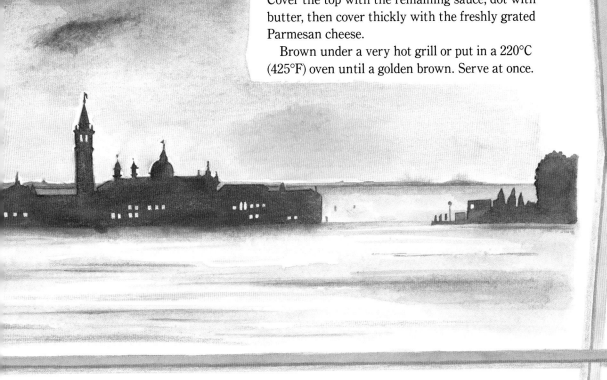

MOULDED PASTA WITH MEAT, CHEESE AND AUBERGINE (EGGPLANT)

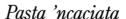

Pasta 'ncaciata

2 large aubergines (eggplants)
Salt
Black pepper
30 mL (2 tablespoons) olive oil
2 cloves garlic, finely chopped
150 g (5 oz) lean pork or veal,
    chopped
3 slices salami, chopped
500 mL (16 fl oz) fresh tomato
    sauce (see page 8)
Oil for deep frying eggplants
    (aubergines)
500 g (1 lb) rigatoni
200 g (7 oz) fresh cheese
    (primosale, tuma or
    mozzarella), sliced
3 hard boiled eggs, sliced
100 g (3½ oz) pecorino or
    Parmesan cheese, freshly grated

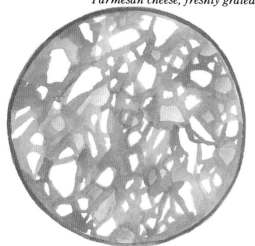

THIS TASTY AND SUBSTANTIAL dish is a meal in itself. If required, it can be prepared in advance and baked just before you are ready to serve. Although in Sicily it is traditionally made with meat, it works equally well without the meat and salami.

Method: Cut the unpeeled aubergines (eggplants) into thin slices, sprinkle with salt and leave for an hour to purge the bitter juices. Heat the olive oil, gently brown the garlic and discard. Brown the meat on all sides and add the tomato sauce. Cook gently for 30 minutes. Rinse and dry the aubergine (eggplant) slices then deep-fry them a few at a time. Drain them on paper towels.

Grease a deep round oven dish and line the sides and bottom with overlapping slices of aubergine (eggplant), reserving a few slices for the top of the mould.

Cook the pasta in boiling salted water until it is half cooked then drain. Stir the meat and tomato sauce into the pasta. Put a layer of pasta in the dish and cover with some slices of cheese. Then make another layer of pasta covered with sliced eggs. The third layer of pasta is covered with the salami and slices of cheese. Cover the last layer of pasta with the remaining aubergine (eggplant). Sprinkle a good layer of grated cheese on top and bake at 190°C (375°F) for 20 minutes. Remove from the oven and leave to stand for 10 minutes. Cover with an inverted serving plate and turn upside down to unmould. The remaining grated cheese is served separately.

TEMPLE OF CONCORD · AGRIGENTO · SICILY

BAKED CAPELLINI WITH HAM AND MOZZARELLA

Capellini al forno con proscuitto e mozzarella

50 g (1½ oz) breadcrumbs
3 eggs
Salt
Black pepper
500 g (1 lb) capellini
100 g (3½ oz) freshly grated
    Parmesan cheese
100 g (3½ oz) butter, melted
150 g (5 oz) Parma ham, thinly
    sliced
300 g (9½ oz) mozzarella cheese,
    thinly sliced

ANY PASTA CAN be used to make this recipe but it works best with thin pasta. Most of the recipe can be prepared in advance then finished off with the topping and cooked just before you eat.

Method: Butter a shallow oven dish and sprinkle with half the breadcrumbs. Beat the eggs with a little salt and pepper. Cook the pasta in boiling salted water, drain, and stir in three-quarters of the Parmesan cheese and three-quarters of the butter. Put half the pasta into the oven dish and cover with the ham and mozzarella cheese slices. Pour over the eggs and then add the rest of the pasta. Sprinkle with the remaining breadcrumbs, Parmesan and butter. Bake in an oven at 250°C (500°F) until golden brown. Serve at once.

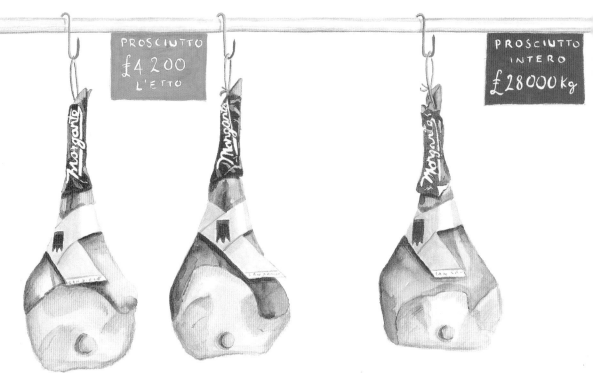

PROSCIUTTO
£4200
L'ETTO

PROSCIUTTO
INTERO
£28000 kg

BAKED RIGATONI WITH FENNEL, CREAM AND HAM

Rigatoni al forno con salsa di finocchi e prosciutto cotto

500 g (1 lb) fennel bulbs
Salt
100 mL (3½ fl oz) fresh cream
Black pepper
30 mL (2 tablespoons) olive oil
30 g (1 oz) butter
150 g (5 oz) diced, cooked ham
500 g (1 lb) rigatoni
50 g (1½ oz) freshly grated
    Parmesan cheese

THIS PASTA CAN BE prepared in advance and put in the oven just before you are ready to eat.

Method: Remove the feathery tubes and any tough fibres from the fennel. Roughly chop two-thirds into slices and cook until tender in lightly salted boiling water. Drain and purée. Stir in the cream and season to taste. Cut the remaining fennel into small cubes and cook gently in the oil and butter for 15 minutes, then add the diced ham. Season to taste. Half cook the pasta in boiling salted water, drain and stir in the cream sauce, followed by the ham and fennel mixture. Turn into a shallow greased oven dish and sprinkle with the freshly grated Parmesan cheese. Add some freshly ground black pepper and cook in an oven at 200°C (400°F) for 15 to 20 minutes. Serve at once.

ACKNOWLEDGEMENTS

I would like to thank Dr Antonio Capalbi who has shared
my culinary explorations over the years, and all my friends
in Italy who have helped my research for this book.

Sarah Hocombe's illustrations capture the special magic
of Italian life, and I would like to thank her for her romantic
imagination and sensitive interpretation of my feelings
for Italy.

At Simon & Schuster, I am grateful for Elenie Poulos's
tireless editing skills and Kirsty Melville's determination
to make it all happen.

INDEX